The Death of the American University

THE DEATH
of the
AMERICAN UNIVERSITY

With Special Reference to the
Collapse of City College of New York

L. G. HELLER

ARLINGTON HOUSE *New Rochelle, N.Y.*

Library of Congress Catalog Card Number 72–91214

ISBN 0–87000–185–X

MANUFACTURED IN THE UNITED STATES OF AMERICA

To Alice

"Send a cheer to Heaven ringing,
Voicing in a fond acclaim
Faith and pride in Alma Mater
And her never dying fame."

—from "Lavender, My Lavender,"
the anthem of the City College
of New York, words written by
Elias Lieberman, Class of 1903

Contents

Preface

From time to time most major institutions undergo reconsideration, revision, and varying degrees of reorganization. Such evolution is a natural and appropriate reaction to changing times and changing needs. Nevertheless, at the present moment the American educational establishment is being subjected to massive and vicious attacks that differ in kind as well as in degree from any which have occurred before. To those who are abreast of the developments, the clear and evident intent is not a changed but improved system: it is the total destruction of the system itself, together with the society which relies upon it.

Among the true scholars and dedicated educators who have grasped the dimensions of what is taking place, there has arisen a despair that transcends simple description. Some such men, whose whole lives have been involved with the classroom, their students, and their books, have asserted that they hope they can last out the few more years they need for retirement. Others, not in the system long enough to be entitled to a pension, are looking for practical ways to get out. In a few rare but grievous instances, great teachers have actually committed suicide as a result of their disillusionment and heartache. Their whole world—their way of life, the values that they cherish—would seem to be crumbling. During the last year or two, the increased number of fatal or near fatal strokes and heart attacks among college professors bears a direct correlation with the tensions engendered by the new circumstances.

The author of this book, who has spent an entire lifetime in the world of scholarship—first as a student for twenty-six years (including ten years at graduate school to the doctoral or post-doctoral level in three fields), then as a teacher, and occasionally as an administrator—refuses to surrender without a struggle. This volume, therefore, constitutes the author's own analysis of the present situation and some suggestions for rectifying it. Surely the greatness of our nation rests in large part on the type of men and women turned out by the educational system. As rightly understood by the enemies of the country, if that system is destroyed, the downfall of America itself is imminent. Consequently there can and must be no retreat, no craven capitulation to the anarchists, Communists, and know-nothings who would bring down our society.

All of the events depicted in this book are true. Nothing has been made up, although much of the material will undoubtedly strike the reader as fiction-like in quality, some episodes resembling perhaps the theater of the absurd. Nevertheless, the author who has either personally lived through many of the happenings or has spoken directly to the principals or eyewitnesses of the events is fully prepared to prove, if need be, the truth of the allegations in a court of law. Most of the events chosen to illustrate the major points of this book have taken place at the City College of New York, where the author teaches. Occasional additions describe similar or related events which have occurred elsewhere—Stanford, Cornell, Princeton, and so on. The City College focus, however, should not be seen as provincial in nature. With only minor differences in specific details, the same attack on the higher educational system is taking place throughout the country—perhaps throughout the world. Were it not for this fact, the author might well have been tempted merely to say goodbye to City College and go to teach elsewhere. Yet no institution in the United States is immune to the same internal and external pressures. The author has seen friends and colleagues pull up stakes and move to other universities in the hope of avoiding intolerable situations only to find that the trouble they had sought to avoid had preceded them to their new posts. One such friend of the author has started to consider seriously how he can give up teaching completely.

In the pages which follow, details are given and specific names are named. In a relatively few instances only initials—or, alternatively, made-up names—are used to protect certain individuals from reprisals or to avoid persecuting others whose self-inflicted suffering from the knowledge that they have acted shamefully, out of cowardice and expediency, is already great enough without singling them out for further public reproach. Nevertheless their stories should be told as a lesson to others. Undoubtedly, with only the most trifling changes of minor detail, the same stories could be told of other individuals. Indeed, this point calls to mind the comment of the ancient Roman poet Horace, who once asked, "Cur fabulam meam rides? Nomine mutato, de te fabula narratur." ("Why do you laugh at my story? With the name changed, the story is told about you.")

One final comment is necessary. Although to the reader who has not had access to true reports of what has been occurring the piling of unhappy detail on detail may appear overwhelming, the simple fact is that the author has made only a limited selection from the countless events which have taken place. The episodes selected are illustrative, not exhaustive. A full recounting of what occurred would require an army of researchers. Nevertheless it is hoped that even the comparatively brief presentation will move at least some readers to action. Not just the educational establishment, but the country itself cries out for help.

It would be difficult for the author to acknowledge adequately the debt this book owes to the many scholars whose comments and discussions have sharpened the author's insights and, occasionally, have provided details or corrected matters of fact. Chief among these colleagues and consultants are the following: at the City College of New York, Professor Howard Adelson, the former chairman of the History Department; Professor Marnin Feinstein of the Department of Classical Languages and Hebrew, and his wife Marcia; Professor Gerald Sirkin of the Department of Economics, who graciously let the author see excerpts from his daily diary for much of the period relevant to this book, and Professor Sirkin's wife Natalie; and Professor Nathan Süsskind, of the Department of Germanic and Slavic Languages. Professor Judah Adelson of the Department of History of the State University at New Paltz likewise served as a patient sounding board and has helped in innumerable ways. Although discussions with Professor Miro Todorovich, the Secretary of the University Centers for Rational Alternatives, were less frequent than the author would have preferred, they never failed to put events into perspective. Thanks are also due to Professor James Macris, of Clark University and the College of the Holy Cross, who has collaborated with the author on many books and whose extended discussions, sharp memory for precise detail, and shrewd judgment have been invaluable. Thanks are likewise owing to Norman Young, a friend and advisor, who has provided secretarial and other assistance through his business office and whose kind encouragement has helped induce the author to complete this book and several others. Last, but most assuredly not least, is Alice Heller, to whom this book is dedicated, who has typed portions, transported, fetched, copied, listened, read, commented, and generally worried greatly lest the telling of this story evoke vast punitive reprisals upon the author. (See in particular the chapter "On Speaking Up in Academia.") Unfortunately—or fortunately—there is a righteous indignation which transcends either prudence or fear. Nonetheless, her loving concern has not gone unnoticed, and this note and the dedication acknowledge that fact.

Part One

CRISIS

1. Violence on Campus

When Professor Robert Hennion of the City College Department of Classical Languages went to his colleague's assistance, the seven black militants transferred their attack to him. Wrestling him to the ground, they proceeded to kick and stomp him, evidently with every intention of killing him. Professor Hennion, a big man, buried his head in his arms, but, nevertheless, his face and hands were cut and bleeding. Fortunately, a brave young Greek student leaped in and, almost unaided, managed to break up the deadly assault until additional assistance came.

Across the hall, where Joseph Wohlberg, an older man in the same department, had been teaching his mythology course, some of his students formed a protective barrier around him, and escorted him out the rear exit of the building to safety. A quiet, scholarly person, who suffered from colitis, Wohlberg was not to be well again for months, but he later, bravely, carried on his classes in a room which he obtained in a church after the South Campus came under siege.

Upstairs, Professor Lotte Kohler, a slender, pleasant woman, was teaching German to a few girls, when the militants burst into her room. Deeming resistance futile with only the girls for protection, she was ready to leave at once, but the militants drenched her and her students with foam from a fire extinguisher. Fleeing up the stairs, while the girls scattered in panic, Dr. Kohler took refuge, together with the secretary of the department, in a room with an iron door, which the two women locked. They tried to telephone for help, but the outside telephone lines were severed. They could only hope the door would hold.

Professor Michael Rywkin, of the same department, was about to teach his Russian literature course, when first SDS* whites and then black militants entered his room, intent on disruption. A tall, powerful man, Rywkin spread his arms and propelled the belligerents out the door before they realized what was happening. The militants got a metal pipe and shattered the window on the door, nearly catching him in the face with bits of flying glass. According to Rywkin, a Burns guard watched the activity but made no move to help. Before the hostile group could break in, another band set off the fire alarm in the building, and students streamed through the halls. Outside on the lawn, numerous fights broke out. Many students and faculty had to be given emergency treatment at nearby Knickerbocker Hospital. One student's nose was crushed by a lead pipe wielded by a revolutionary.

Professor Richard Plant later started home, taking the longer route through the North Campus, because he deemed it safer. He was accosted just outside the subway station at 145th Street. "Do you teach at City College?"

When he answered, "Yes," two bearded, hippie-clad, SDS whites seized him roughly and pitched him headfirst down the concrete stairs. It was to be weeks before he could recover sufficiently to inquire if he had been in the City University system long enough to allow him to retire. Informed that he still needed another two years, he groaned in pain and despair. He didn't know how he would survive. He had experienced similar occurrences in Germany in 1933.

Sporadic fires arose in many of the college's buildings, and the beautiful Aronow Auditorium became a raging conflagration, impos-

*The initials SDS stand for "Students for a Democratic Society," but, as has been pointed out time and again, these "students"—if they are students—want anything but a democratic society. They are intent primarily on destroying by force the society that exists and imposing their own will on it, but still without any positive, constructive goal beyond the violence itself. Their manner of operation reflects a fascistic organization rather than a democratic one.

sible to extinguish before the building had been thoroughly gutted, rendered not merely unusable but actually a safety menace, as the walls could topple at any time.

Many professors could not even leave the troubles behind at school. Anonymous phone calls threatened them and their families. The chairman of the History Department, Professor Howard Adelson, who had seen active combat service as an officer in two wars, did not fear for himself, but he was to become afraid to have his ten-year-old son Mark answer the phone, since an unknown caller took satisfaction in telling the boy that his father was going to be murdered.

The full story of what happened at City College in that terrible Spring of 1969 will probably never be told. It would, in any event, take a different kind of book than the present one, which is concerned not with City College as City College but with what happened at City College and elsewhere as symptoms of a more serious problem, one which is taking many forms. The entire educational structure is under attack from without and within. Furthermore it shows every indication of succumbing to that attack, at least in certain very essential ways.

2. The Takeover

It was April 23, the anniversary of William Shakespeare's birth and death (in 1564 and 1616 respectively), a time more appropriate to scholarly pursuits or discrete academic reminiscing. Most of the college community was following its customary schedule in a business-as-usual fashion, with no suspicion of the gathering cataclysm about to change for all time the very nature of the well-ordered, intellectual way of life central to academia. Term papers were soon due, and final examinations were just weeks away. Students and faculty alike felt the gratified weariness that accompanies the end of the academic year as the spring term moved into its final phase. Graduation was little more than a month away for some. The first robins were hopping about on the lawn, and the early-blooming forsythia was still green, with touches of yellow presaging the golden blaze to come.

In the Administration Building, the Committee on Curriculum and Teaching had just gathered for its usual Tuesday meeting, striving to resolve the last flurry of problems, as various departments hastened to get their new courses into the program for the following year. Someone entered the room and whispered to Professor Waldhorn, the chairman of the committee. He asked a question and received a murmured reply.

"Gentlemen," said Waldhorn, "some black and Puerto Rican students have seized South Campus. An emergency meeting of the faculty is being held in Room 200, Shepard. I suggest that we adjourn and attend that meeting."

Dean Barber protested. "If we don't get the items on the agenda out of the way today, we'll never finish our schedule."

"I for one want to see if we're going to have a schedule to complete before I deal with the curricular matters," said Waldhorn.

Several other members of the committee expressed their views, with the dean adamantly defending the need to stay and do the regular work. A vote resolved the problem, and the members disbanded, some to attend the faculty meeting, others to go about their own pursuits. Dean Barber shook his head in annoyance. He still hadn't grasped the enormity of what was happening. Eventually he was to resign his administrative post as a result of the events then being set in motion. Centuries of tradition were crumbling, but at the moment only the first symptoms were showing—and it was precisely the business-as-usual attitude and the clinging to outmoded, inappropriate ways of handling crisis that helped undermine that which *was* valid in the academic way of life.

The emergency meeting was already in progress as faculty members straggled in from various parts of the campus. Although the gathering appeared to be a hastily convened group of concerned faculty, there was later to be some suspicion that at least a few of the professors must have known more than they indicated. Certainly, particular individuals who worked almost in unison and expressed a particular point of view were to serve in days to come as consultants to the militant students and to try to force complete capitulation to all of the demands. On this occasion, they got up one after another to insist that police must *not* be called. They attacked as reactionary anyone who expressed a different view. The fact that the rights of thousands of students were being trampled in the interest of publicizing the demands of only forty or fifty students did not weigh very heavily in the reckoning. This rejection of legitimate aid from a public law enforcement group—a holdover from a medieval struggle between university and secular authorities—was to be the single most disastrous policy followed. It later became clear that the militants had expected the police to be called. Furthermore they had been quite prepared to leave quietly when the police arrived. Instead, the faculty decided not to call the police. Thus, (1) the militants barricaded behind locked gates on South Campus brought the operation of the entire college to a halt, and (2) the ensuing publicity, with press and television coverage, made heroes out of them. As written up by the reporters, the protesters were fighting for equality, justice, and the American way of life against a racist monolithic organization. The absurdity of calling City College racist is—or should be—patent to anyone who knows the history of the institution, which was founded explicitly so that the children of the rich and the poor would sit together in the same classroom, with no distinctions of race, color, religion, or creed. Also, the discrepancy between the stated goals and the real goals of the hard-core militants only emerged later. This problem, which lies at the heart of almost all of the inappropriate reactions of faculty and administrators throughout the country, will form the focus of a later section of this book. For the moment, suffice it to say that the real goal was the *destruction* of "the capitalist, imperialist, racist society." It is true that *some* of the protesters were actually aiming at the substance of the five demands—perfectly legitimate and reasonable, with a few minor modifications—but the stipulated reasons were *not* what motivated the real instigators of the lockout. Although the truth of this allegation would be difficult to prove in a court of law because of the intimidation of potential witnesses, there is reason to believe that some of the blacks who raised valid questions regarding the demands were brutally beaten to shut them up. Also the author of this book knows of some black students who did *not* want to use violence but who were forced into line. One of those students later risked his own life to warn the author of this book of a threat to murder him because he would not complacently submit to the establishment of a school for revolution. (More will be said of this point also.)

Dr. Buell Gallagher, the president of the college, who had been out of town, arrived in the middle of the meeting. He asked for guidance from the faculty. The members advised him to close the college for that day—it was already late afternoon—and possibly for the next, so as to have time for consultation and negotiation. *The college was to remain closed until private individuals, acting on their own, forced it, via an injunction, to reopen.* Gallagher himself was to be forced out of his post as a result of this decision and what ensued. The real question is that of why Gallagher asked the faculty to make a decision that was his and his alone. The faculty has its areas of decision-making, but the determination to close the college is not one of them. However, Gallagher was faced with the same problem that *still* confronts every high-ranking educational administrator in the country—the undermining of his authority both by faculty and students, occasionally with some collusion, and usually for various unrelated reasons. Gallagher's confidence in his own authority had already been undermined some time prior to that of his abdication of responsibility. Yet the responsibility he refused to take—oh how prudent he thought he was at the moment—led to his academic demise. This fact was unfortunate, for Dr. Gallagher was a decent, well-meaning human being. In normal circumstances he was even a capable, efficient administrator. However, the times have changed, and the academic establishment needs a new breed of supervisor—one which can boldly make the decisions that have to be made and tell the critics where to go—even help them along, for *no matter what decision is made under the new arrangements the administrator will be attacked.*

3. The Undermining of Authority

The faculty and administrators of the City College of New York had watched the events, first at Berkeley, then at Columbia University, in fascinated horror, regarding the transactions in much the same vein as they would regard pages from the theater of the absurd. "Terrible," they thought, "but what has this to do with us?" They could not conceive of anything similar happening at CCNY. Such a possibility was quite remote. In their certainty, they failed to recognize the first probing of the authoritarian structure and moral fiber on which every large educational institution necessarily rests. *Their* reactions set the stage for the eventual demise of the college as a serious educational enterprise of integrity and high standards.

At Columbia the pretext had been the erection, at university expense, of a gymnasium for the use of the neighborhood youth. This wicked deed had sufficed to show the faculty, students, and interested observers the vicious nature of the "racist, capitalistic imperialistic institution," an excellent reason for destroying one of the world's foremost universities. At City College the first pretext was not so imposing as a gymnasium extending a quarter of an acre into the surrounding community. No, indeed. City College was trying desperately to meet the needs—not luxuries—of the city it had served for so long. Space had to be found to accommodate an increased enrollment. The fiction of Mark Hopkins and his pupil sitting side by side on a log while discussing philosophy or literature is romantic and entertaining, but when snow lies on the ground the log is hardly conducive to the teaching of large numbers of students.

As an interim expedient, until new buildings already planned could be erected, the administration decided to put up some temporary Quonset-hut-like structures which could be razed when space became available elsewhere. The beneficiaries of the new plan would, by and large, be the younger brothers and sisters of the students already at college.

Suddenly a major protest arose. A group of radical students had discovered that City College was rotten to the core: it was about to chop down *three trees* to make room for the temporary buildings. At once bearded hippies, wearing no shirts but carrying loudspeakers attached to expensive electronic amplifying systems, appeared from nowhere, to begin haranguing the slowly gathering crowds about the virtues of those venerable trees and about the crafty nature of the administration which was plotting behind the students' backs to deprive them of their national heritage. Many academicians were inclined to regard the proceedings as an elaborate joke. Surely no one would seriously consider depriving hundreds of young men and women of the right to a free education so as to preserve three trees.

The earnestness of the protesters' intent became evident, however, when workmen arrived on campus to push through the project in order to have the buildings ready for use when needed. Militant students lay down in the path of bulldozers, occupied the foundation trenches so that the concrete could not be poured, and generally blocked every effort to proceed. When Dr. Gallagher tried to reason with them, they reviled him in no uncertain terms. Rallies were held at both the North and South Campuses. At some of the meetings on South Campus, students could be seen dangling from the branches of a couple of those very trees whose health and well being were serving as the pretext for the probing of the administrative will. Still many faculty and administrators could not quite grasp the deadly game whose opening gambit had started.

The first meetings focused on the trees, but later larger gatherings began to display evidence of Marxist revolutionary rhetoric, with touches of Mao and Che Guevara. The early rallies had almost a festive, holiday note. The sun glinted bright on the grass-covered lawns; the warmth of spring was in the air. Boys and girls carried on harmless flirtations. In the background, however, was the sometimes sophisticated, sometimes naive rhetoric of dedicated revolutionists. If these activists, later to become far more skillful in their presentations, were often clumsy, their audiences hardly possessed the perspicacity to reply appropriately. To a great extent many of the students attending these first skirmishes—they were no less than that—were of the apolitical variety—decent, hardworking, goodnatured. The first meetings superficially resembled more traditional panty-raid or athletic-rally types that had served for centuries to provide a pleasant, harmless channel for excess spirits and energy. The stated objective—the preservation of trees on campus—gave just enough plausibility to the activities to profit by the earliest ripples of the gathering ecology movement. The confrontation tactic devoted to the complete closing down of the colleges had not yet been invoked, but absenteeism was increasing, as rallies coincided with class hours.

One gum-chewing, exuberant seventeen-year-old girl with braces on her teeth asked her teacher if she could cut class to attend a rally in front of the Cohen Library. "It's all so exciting," she bubbled.

Her teacher replied that she *always* had the option of failing her courses if she wanted to. Somewhat crestfallen, the girl went to class, much as though she had been denied the right to attend a graduation party or a formal dance.

Some of the revolutionary rhetoric, skillfully injected into the speeches, began to have an effect. The crowds became larger; the audiences, sullen or hostile. Faculty members going to get their cars which were parked in the vicinity of South Campus lawn encountered belligerent students seated on the roofs and hoods of their vehicles. Instead of scampering off, the squatters muttered oaths and displayed resentment when asked to move. A few of the women faculty were frightened, and occasionally men on the staff accompanied them when they went to get their automobiles.

Eventually, of course, the impasse had to be broken lest the college be forced to turn away would-be students. After a last appeal, then, Dr. Gallagher called for the police, who arrested those students seated in the ditches dug for the concrete foundations. Some of the protestors were dragged off, kicking, and screaming foulmouthed obscenities.

Immediately faculty and students—that is *some* faculty and *some* students—were up in arms over the decision to call in the police. Gallagher had allowed all the time he had had available for the protestors to register their objections to the erection of the buildings and the concomitant removal of the trees. As the chief administrator at the college he had had no option left whatsoever. Even his offer to try to replant the trees had had no effect. Clearly, of course, the real intent of the hard-core militants had been totally unrelated to the stated cause of the objections.Nevertheless, funds were collected to hire legal counsel for the activists who now faced serious consequences. Many faculty still did not see these students as revolutionists. There was a "boys-will-be-boys" attitude.

The police-on-campus issue became a *cause célèbre*. Eventually the entire faculty was to meet to debate the issue. Then a motion was made by a small group of faculty members (who had administrative ambitions and were delighted by the chance to embarrass the president) that Gallagher be stripped of his right to call the police. Faculty rhetoric ran high, and somehow the central core of the revolutionists' real goals disappeared in the noises made relating to academic freedom—as though the calling of law enforcement agents constituted a threat to academic freedom.

A compromise was offered that Gallagher be forced to consult a joint committee of faculty and students before being allowed to call police. Such a motion would clearly be meaningless, not to mention illegal. The faculty *could not* take away the responsibilities of the college president: only the Board of Higher Education could do that. Furthermore, as the author of this book pointed out rather heatedly on that occasion, what would happen in the event of genuine trouble? Not all of us had been blind to the violence that was beginning to escalate at other campuses throughout the country. What if some militant group decided to burn down the college? Did the faculty propose to tie Gallagher's hands anyway? Consider the consequences. Dr Gallagher, on being notified that some militants were beginning to burn Finley Hall, would say, "Take a letter, Miss Ryan. Send it to the Joint Committee of Students and Faculty on Calling the Police. Invite them to meet—oh, say next Thursday—we'll need at least that much time for the letters to reach them. Oh, by the way, Miss Ryan. Figure out where they can meet. I hear that the students are burning down both the Administration Building and Shepard Hall also, so we won't be able to assemble in any of the normal meeting places."

The absurdity of the motion was evident. Nevertheless the proposal was put to the vote. Dr. Gallagher himself was presiding. Now Buell Gallagher, a Protestant minister, was a polite gentleman with a standard of conduct, a code of chivalry, that is totally out of place in a dog-eat-dog, every-man-for-himself kind of age. Had he been a different sort of person, he would have ruled the motion out of order. Had he also been a modern administrator, he would have then taken steps to get rid of those faculty members who were out to "get" him—hoping, no doubt, to inherit his soon-to-be-vacant post or at least one close to it. Instead Dr. Gallagher allowed the vote to be taken by a *voice* count. To this (admittedly not impartial) witness the ayes and the nays seemed about equal. Bending backward in a gallant but absurd chivalric gesture, Dr. Gallagher ruled that "The ayes have it." He was showing how eminently fair he was. In so doing, he set the stage for the future destruction of the college.* Those who had voted "no" to the proposal were stunned. (a) How could he have allowed the vote at all? (b) How could he have ruled either way on such a close vote? Gallagher's gesture did not impress his enemies in the slightest: they saw it as stupidity, not magnanimity. It did, however, demoralize his supporters, who were stupefied. If anyone but Gallagher himself had been in the chair, they would have called

*The folly of any impressionistic reliance on the volume of sound in any close vote by voice may be seen in what happened on another—later—occasion, when Dr. Joseph Copeland, who was to succeed Dr. Gallagher, occupied the chair as presiding officer. One faculty radical, who regularly voted in a booming voice, demanded a recount after Dr. Copeland had ruled that the motion had been defeated. Commenting on the waste of time, Dr. Copeland took a more precise tabulation by hand vote. The result not only confirmed his own earlier judgment rather than that of the protester, but it revealed that the balloting hadn't even been close. Dr. Copeland commented, "You see, Mr. Schulman, a loud vote still counts as only one vote."

for a count by hands or even for written ballots. Indeed, it would have been better for their cause—and ultimately the cause of higher education generally—if an avowed anarchist or Communist had been presiding. Then they would have known what to do. As things were, they remained silent and lost the vote. Gallagher—a good Christian—had turned the other cheek, but it had been *their* cheeks, not merely his own which he had turned. Gallagher had sown the wind; the whirlwind was about to follow. Again, it must be emphasized, the faculty vote, whatever its moral force, could not be and was not legally binding. Short of resignation, Gallagher could not avoid his own personal responsibility as the president of City College.

The next crisis came over an AWOL soldier, Bill Brakefield, who sought sanctuary at the college. The concept of sanctuary dates from the Middle Ages when the churches had acquired freedom from secular molestation, thus allowing the ecclesiastical authorities to shield those of their own faith (or of other faiths if the church fathers cared to extend their protection) from irreligious persecutors. The sanctuary concept was a practical test of the separation of church and state. It was won at bitter cost. Unless one saw City College as a religion or church, however, the application of the sanctuary right hardly applied here. That some faculty members did see the college in such a role appears likely. Furthermore they cast themselves in the parts of the high priests of the faith.

The year was 1968—a time before the Kent State episode, before My Lai, and before the full tide of opposition to the Vietnamese war. The radical student groups saw the pathetic figure of the soldier as a good focal point to crystalize firm rebellion both to the federal government and to the college authorities. In fact the situation was made to order for the purpose: the college authorities might choose to support the government in shipping the soldier back for punishment and/or military service. If so, the college authorities could be held up to scorn as part of the military-industrial complex—a political line that was to be taken very successfully at a later date by the dissident groups. Alternatively, the college authorities might choose to defy the federal government—an unlikely possibility then, but one which would split both authorities and drive a wedge between them with devastating consequences. As before, many of the students—those who were not members of the SDS or other antiestablishment organizations—could be reached by an effective appeal to their sympathies.

The militant groups surrounded the soldier in Finley Hall and prepared to do battle with all comers. A twenty-four hour vigil was set up to protect the deserter. Again a carnival atmosphere prevailed, analogous perhaps to that of a circus or an athletic stadium prior to a contest. Instead of popcorn or frankfurters, however, narcotics flowed freely. When Dr. Gallagher appeared on the scene to try to reason with the students that the college could not legitimately be used to defy the federal government, he received jeers and insults. Some of the students had smeared the walls of the room with obscene slogans written in glaring paints. Others ignored him and made love in the aisles. The license taken went beyond simple impropriety. According to Gallagher, some of the couples were actually fornicating in full public view on the tables. Still others started to pile up wooden furniture, heap up kerosene-impregnated rags in mounds, slash the fire hoses, and otherwise make gestures suggestive of intended arson.

Dean Peace, after conferring with Gallagher, called the local police, thus in effect defying the faculty. Dr. Gallagher appeared most indignant about the fornication and obscene signs. The evidence of the intended arson was all but disregarded. At that time few of the faculty or administration were ready to believe the violent, destructive intent of the militants. Yet, as indicated, less than a year later Aronow Auditorium was to burn and dozens of other fires to sweep the campus. As was predictable, large numbers of the faculty were incensed over the calling of the police. More than that, the Faculty Council met in angry session. Resolutions condemning Dr. Gallagher and Dean Peace were proposed. Again acting the part of a scrupulously fair administrator, Dr. Gallagher withdrew from the chair as presiding officer while the discussion and voting took place. The debate was stormy and acrimonious. A small faction was determined to embarrass the president, but many of the faculty, still recognizing him as a decent, considerate human being, were unwilling to allow him to be censured publicly. Yet a censure of Dean Peace would in effect be a censure of Dr. Gallagher. Therefore, in the separate balloting the vote went against Dr. Peace. The count split in the vote to censure Gallagher himself, but that resolution failed by a close vote. Ironically, had Gallagher himself remained in the chair, he might have allowed a voice count: undoubtedly he would have ruled against himself. As it was, Dean Peace was sacrificed as a compromise to an avowed repudiation of the college president.

It still remains a mystery as to how the council expected the administrators to fulfill their obligations as administrators. Clearly a small faction whose opinions unfortunately carried a good deal of weight with other faculty members were out to displace Gallagher so that they or their friends could take over the running of the college. Still other faculty members reacted almost irrationally to the no-police-on-campus cliche; others saw the administrative move as part of a continuing conflict between faculty and administration, as though their ultimate goals were necessarily antithetical. With the possible exception, however, of some radical, anarchistic members of the faculty who later shifted their main activities to agitation for revolution, few of the professors grasped as yet the long-term impact of their shortsighted move.

Under the circumstances, any self-respecting administrator had to recognize that either (1) he must be prepared to defy the faculty as often as necessary, regardless of their censure, or (2) he must resign. One could not go running to the entire faculty every time a crisis arose—and crises were to become the daily norm within a short period of time. Dean Peace *did* resign not long thereafter. Gallagher thought he could still steer a moderate course, appeasing everyone. His view was wrong; just how wrong, however, was not to be evident for some time. The net effect of the vote of censure was to rob the administration of any confidence in its ability or even right to shoulder its own responsibilities.

4. Administrative Default

Once it becomes evident that in a crisis no administrator can expect support for *any* decision he may make, many men of reasonable prudence but limited moral fiber predictably take the easiest path rather than the one which is best for the institution entrusted to their guidance. Normally this path is that of appeasement of or capitulation to the militant groups, despite the fact that such spinelessness frequently involves direct injustice to others, whether faculty or students. Such an administrator lives from crisis to crisis on a day-to-day basis. If he has thoughts of the long-range consequences of his expediency, he suppresses them in the interest of sparing himself the unpleasantness of the most imminent confrontation. He relies on the good will of the victims of his lack of fortitude, trusting that they, unlike, the militants, will not burn down a building or hit him over the head. Consider, for example, the following cases.

Dr. Carlos Stoetzer, a scholarly professor of history chosen with painstaking care from among over fifty applicants for the position,* found himself at odds with a very militant faction of his History-of-Puerto Rico class. Apparently his way of presenting the details did not accord with their nationalistic aspirations. The fact that presum-

*According to his departmental chairman, Dr. Stoetzer, a former member of the faculty of Fordham University, had been "chosen in large measure because, in addition to his scholarly competence, it was felt that he would be most useful in advancing the careers of the students because of his wide acquaintance with the men in the field. . . . Stoetzer was an Argentinian."

ably he, not the students, had the training, perspective, and qualifications to judge the relative weight of emphasis to be given to different parts of the presentation, played no role at all in what happened. One day he appeared in his assigned room only to be met by jeers, insults, threats, and—weapons. One "student" had a large knife fastened to a bamboo pole. This young man punctuated his comments by bangs of the improvised implement on the teacher's desk. The scholar bravely held his ground but had to halt the lesson for the day.

When he reported the facts to Professor Howard Adelson, his departmental chairman, the latter passed on the information to the Dean of Students and to the Dean of the College of Liberal Arts and Science, and demanded protection for Professor Stoetzer. He made it clear that he would not allow the faculty member back into the classroom unless such protection were provided. The two deans assured Adelson that such protection would be made available. Although fuming at the indignities to which Professor Stoetzer has been subjected, the chairman went home for the weekend, satisfied that he had done what he had been able to do in order to safeguard the life of a fine teacher. Needless to say, he told Professor Stoetzer that no repetition of the unpleasant incident could take place.

The following Monday, Professor Stoetzer returned to his classroom ready to do the job for which he had been so well trained. He expected Burns guards to be present, whether overtly or covertly, as well as a representative of the administration, to guarantee his safety. No such protective group was in evidence. Instead, a rowdy, hostile band of about twenty accusers, including some who were not students, awaited him. They launched into a diatribe against him. He said that either they would have to leave or else he would. They refused. The language they directed at him was both obscene and provocative. Fully expecting to be assaulted physically, Professor Stoetzer fled to a nearby office, still pursued by the militants directing their belligerency at him. He later filed charges with the city police.

As soon as the deans who had reneged on their promise heard of the legal action, they tried to force Professor Stoetzer to withdraw his complaint—to grant amnesty. The latter refused. It had been *his* life that had been threatened and *his* rights that had been abridged.

The departmental chairman supported Stoetzer's position and, further, demanded an explanation of why Professor Stoetzer had not received the protection he had been led to expect. Dr. Adelson also called for a disciplinary hearing. The dean of the college suddenly shifted his position. After all, he asserted, how could he know who was in the right, Professor Stoetzer or the students? Besides, he had been told that Professor Stoetzer had directed a bad word against the Puerto Ricans. In view of the language employed daily on campus, such a charge was ludicrous. Furthermore, the dean failed to mention the abuse heaped on Professor Stoetzer. He also ignored the seemingly anomalous fact that Professor Stoetzer had *never* been heard to use any but the most polite, courteous language at any time by anyone who knew him. What about the use of the knife, asked the chairman. Surely the dean wasn't going to condone an illegal, not to mention intolerable, threat to a faculty member. Oh, replied the dean, he had been told that the Professor Stoetzer's eyesight must be bad because the student had only had a recorder (a type of flute), not a knife.

The chairman checked back with Professor Stoetzer, who insisted that he recognized a knife when he saw one. The details of what ensued need not concern us here beyond the following. The administration, rather than supporting Professor Stoetzer's right to teach a class in peace, actually attempted to discredit him. They also *refused* to hold any disciplinary hearings. They uncritically repeated the militants' claim that the group which had entered the classroom that second time had actually come with only the most amiable, peaceful intentions to reason with Professor Stoetzer, who, allegedly, had been insulting and abusive to them. The administration pointedly overlooked, however, the relative chronology or the implications of a scurrilous and libelous sheet which had *already* been prepared, mimeographed, distributed, and posted by the group, *prior* to that "peaceful" confrontation. The real basis for the administrative turnabout can be seen in an inadvertent remark by one of the deans, who exclaimed, "and, besides, I don't want to get a brick through *my* window." Professor Stoetzer eventually left the college. Quite apart from the unpleasantness—not to mention the actual danger—of both confrontation and politics rather than discussion and education, it was clear that the administration did not care enough about the rights of the faculty or even about the needs of the peaceful majority of students. Its major concern was its own need to avoid trouble for itself. It would not only capitulate to any militant group ready and willing to make trouble: it would go out of its way to anticipate the wishes of such a group, even if its action involved a disregard or outright denial of the rights of *non*militants. Seemingly, nothing could make it act from morality rather than expediency.

As an addendum to the foregoing story, one may note that Professor Stoetzer's successor, a Cuban who had left his own country because of Castro, promptly came under attack by the militants—for precisely the same reasons. The "students" claimed that only a Puerto Rican could teach Puerto Ricans. The implications of this assumption will be examined elsewhere in this volume.

Another *cause célèbre* arose in the fall term of 1970, when Professor Renee Waldinger, the head of the Department of Romance Languages, suggested an attempt to make the Spanish courses more relevant to the predominantly Puerto Rican Spanish actually spoken in the New York area. Her intent reflected a direct recognition of the importance of the Puerto Rican people and her desire to consider their needs. Accordingly, Professor Gary Keller, one of the teachers in the department, undertook—on his own time and without additional compensation—the task of compiling a glossary of those words and phrases which are peculiar to Puerto Rican Spanish, as apart from other varieties of the Spanish language. He had barely started, having gathered only sixty-eight items, when, seeking aid or correction, he showed his little glossary to other faculty members. He had no intention of publishing the list as yet or even of making it public: he was merely drawing on the expertise and specialized knowledge of his colleagues in the department so as to further the project and make it a useful scholarly, as well as practical, contribution. Suddenly, however, this list "leaked out" to a militant student group, and Keller found himself the target of belligerent accusations that charged him with bigotry. Among other terms, the list contained words such as *maricon,* meaning "homosexual," *moyeto*

("Negro"), *hara* ("police"), and *tecata* ("heroin"). The Puerto Rican Student Union asserted that "the list, which is to be used to educate future teachers, is nothing but a collection of vulgarisms with the sole intent of projecting images of racism, drug addiction, sexual perversity and lawlessness." The group, therefore demanded that Keller be fired at once. To emphasize their point, about twenty of them entered—invaded, perhaps, would be a better word—Keller's class, disrupted the lesson, and refused to leave. Professor Keller, understandably, tried to explain about the list and to defend himself. The group was not interested in what he had to say. Keller's students rose to defend their teacher. One girl, who said that she herself was half Puerto Rican, pointed out that "these are the words we use" and indicated that she didn't understand the basis for the complaint. Another student said that he lived in a Puerto Rican neighborhood and heard these words used by the people around him.

The arguments had no impact. One reporter for the *Observation Post,* a student newspaper, noted that the group disrupting the class contained members of Students for a Democratic Society. He did not have to add that SDS had been responsible for other disruptions in the past and that its real goal had been disruption, not merely the particular pretexts given in each instance. The charge of racism soon extended into a full-scale attack on the Department of Romance Languages, and the Puerto Rican Student Union tacked on five additional demands beyond the original one calling for the dismissal of the teacher. The details of these demands and the substance of the charges need not be considered here. Of greater consequence, the argument later continued at a meeting of the Faculty Senate, where an angry, hostile debate erupted. Some faculty members, including the author of this book, suggested that there were two separate points at issue. The second, *not* the first, was the question of the purported racism. An appropriate fact-finding committee could deal with that. The first point—one which had been arising time and again—was the very serious problem of the frequent disruption of classes by self-appointed groups. Dr. Robert Marshak, the new president of the college, who was chairing the meeting, grew angry when told that it did not seem unreasonable that the administration should see to it that no instructor be interrupted by militant groups, that the maintenance of peace and order in the classrooms should require no special committees or ad hoc resolutions but, rather, should involve automatic, standard regulations and procedures.

In reply, Dr. Marshak argued that "the building of bridges in the academic community" was more important than any professor's right to teach unimpeded and that one needed to convince dissident groups of "our good will." An obvious retort was that an adequate mechanism for the prompt handling of all complaints, including the charge of racism, did not—and should not—depend on violent disruption. Surely the teachers and the peaceful students had some rights too. This answer, however, was not even allowed to be presented. One after another, different faculty members picked up Marshak's theme of building brotherhood and goodwill. They also asserted, in effect, that anyone who insisted on law and order must do so only because he himself was bigoted. Apparently they believed that brotherhood could not go hand in hand with peaceful and orderly procedures. Needless to say, the threat of being accused of bigotry or intolerance prevented many faculty members from expressing their true feelings.

5. The Keller Case in Perspective

As seen, in the attempt to make his courses more "relevant," Dr. Gary Keller had undertaken to compile a specialized glossary which would reflect the lexical differences between Puerto Rican Spanish and that of other origins. Because his study was produced in an atmosphere of high sensitivity to real or imagined slights to citizens of that particular ethnic background and because of his—or their—apparent ignorance of geo- or ethnolinguistic procedures or possibly because the militant group was simply seeking an excuse for disruptive activities, Dr. Keller was subjected both to hostility from his accusers and to suspicion from his professional colleagues, who felt that they had to investigate *every* charge of alleged bias. The governing principle, which supposedly underlies American jurisprudence, namely, that a man is innocent until proven guilty, was ignored. The burden of proof should, by this orientation, have rested on the accusers not the accused. Furthermore the supporting evidence, if any, should have been presented to a genuinely impartial but nevertheless informed judge for an initial determination of whether or not there was even a *prima facie* case worthy of consideration. If these elementary guidelines had been followed, the charge of bias should never have received public recognition at all, not to mention notoriety, with the attendant injury to the accused, his students, and the institution which employs him.

The Faculty Senate of City College, which debated and argued the merits of the case, definitely did not constitute either an impartial or an informed panel for this important function. It was not impartial since it was concerned more for the preservation of its own reputation for good will to minorities than for the need to uphold justice. Thus with *itself,* not the accused, as the unspoken center of consideration, it *ignored*—deliberately ignored—what would have been self-evident to a different jury. This lack of impartiality shades subtly into lack of informed competence to sit in judgment on the merits of *this* case. To put the raw facts into perspective, one may consider an event which took place elsewhere within weeks of the Senate meeting.

The place was the Petit Trianon room of the New York Hilton Hotel; the time, Monday morning, December 28, 1970; the occasion, the annual meeting of the American Dialect Society, a scholarly body of long and distinguished reputation. The speaker was Professor Stanley J. Cook of the California State Polytechnic College, whose talk bore the title, "Examples of Slang Used by Male Juvenile Chicanos in San Bernadino, California: Implications for the Teacher of English."

Professor Cook analyzed a list of thirty-nine words or phrases which *he* had compiled. By his own observation, they represented predominantly the areas of "fighting, sex, and drugs." According to the criterion invoked against Keller, Cook too should have been charged with deliberate misrepresentation, distortion, and bias, in this instance, against Mexican Americans. Clearly, of course, Professor Cook had had no hostile intent in his compilation—most of the terms, in fact, having been volunteered by the youngsters of Mexican background—any more than Keller had had. Yet no one had questioned Cook's motivation or had thought it strange that *his* list had focused on the three dominant areas included. The evidence had simply pointed where it had, but in the absence of any evidence that the investigator had actually made up rather than merely recorded those words which he had encountered, it would never have even occurred to any member of the Dialect Society (which, incidentally, included many eminent scholars of minority-group origin) to question the intent of the scientific investigator. The methodology itself could be questioned; likewise, the conclusions based on the data collected could possibly be called into question—but never the reason for the collection of the raw and as yet undigested data. A major difference, however, lies in the fact that, although the American Dialect Society is a scholarly organization, the City College Faculty Senate—*as a Senate*—is not: it is a political body. Ironically, one member of the Dialect Society, referring to one problem which Cook's list may serve to correct, said that often teachers widen the gulf between themselves and their students "by *not* recognizing the special vocabulary and interests of the minority groups." If so, a City College teacher is in a double bind—damned if he does and damned if he doesn't. Such a situation should not and could not exist if faculty and administrators were more intent on upholding the law with justice rather than with a view to pacifying militants. However, the latter intent is a direct outgrowth of the view, well-established in some quarters, of a university as a place for keeping poorly educated, or uneducated, potential troublemakers from a life of crime rather than a place designed to educate people.

For purposes of perspective, Professor Cook's original hand-out, distributed at the meeting of the society, follows.

**An Illustrative List of Chicano Slang—
San Bernardino Flats**

Bato/vato	fellow, guy.
Bad Juice	descriptive term for an individual good in sports or at fighting.
Bad	cf. *bad juice*, but refers mainly to fighting ability.
Capping	to verbally attack an individual not considered an enemy.
Chota (head)	male sex organ.
Chucie	abbreviation of *Pachuco*, refers to an individual who walks, dresses and acts in a certain way.
(to play) Col	to infringe deliberately on another's feelings.
Cock	girl's vagina.
Fair-fight	used to irritate a teacher.
Frajo	a cigarette.
Gebacho	a white.
Get it	used for drawing attention to a fight, a girl, etc.
Get it on	to urge someone to fight or dance well.
Hammers	girls

Hassle or what	friendly challenge on entering a group.
Heavy	something very good or pleasing, especially music.
In your eye	phrase used to rub in a verbal put-down.
He throws it bad	he thinks he's tough.
(Don't) Jump Bad	a warning not to act aggressively.
Lay it on 'em	a plea to fight well.
Lighten up	a warning to someone who is out of line.
Magoos	sperm
Mean	a complimentary term for a person or object.
Nasty	a complimentary term for an object.
Nelson	an emphatic *no.*
Paddies	teacher's pets (Anglos).
Possums	shoes
Pimping	descriptive term for the way some black males walk.
Puta	a whore.
Puto	a male homosexual.
Ripped	drunk, to get drunk.
Slack	chance or break, as, don't give the guy any slack.
(Let him) Slide	warning not to take advantage of an inferior fighter.
Slyza	shouted after someone scores in a fight or capping session.
Split the Mex	1) to have intercourse or 2) to leave the scene.
(What a) Trip	refers to a lie.
Wicked	complimentary term for an action or object.
Yelson	an emphatic *yes.*
Zeus	shouted when someone has scored a hit in a friendly fight.

Stanley J. Cook
California State Polytechnic
College—Kellogg-Voorhis,
Pomona, California

6. The New Academic Administrator

There was a time when a man of education with some administrative ability could fill the position of college president or dean for as long as his health permitted, and he normally remained until advanced age made retirement mandatory. Yet even this retirement, after a lifetime of service, was one full of honor and respect. The college was his family, and he could watch its continuance and prosperity with affection and satisfaction.

That time has passed. Indeed the sort of person who once became president or dean can no longer cope with the demanding requirements of modern academic administration. A simple knowledge of the mechanics and history of academia and also, for college presidents, of the channels of fund raising, no longer suffices in today's crisis atmosphere. In fact scores of institutions find themselves without key personnel to fill their needs. In previous years a long waiting line of applicants was available for such appointments. Today capable people hesitate before accepting the call to academic administration. The penalties outweigh the satisfactions. Of the few who accept the challenge and responsibility, fewer yet survive for long. Thus, for example, one western institution had five presidents within six months. None could stand the abuse or meet the needs. This situation is typical of that prevailing throughout the country. Even where particular administrators survive, the effect on the institutions can sometimes be seen as disastrous, with one compromise capitulation after another gradually eroding the quality of academic integrity.

One administrator who came into the picture following disastrous demonstrations on campus was Dr. Robert Marshak, formerly of the University of Rochester. An eminent physicist, reputedly chosen because he appeared to favor student power and general participatory governance, he replaced acting-president Dr. Joseph Copeland, who had temporarily superceded Dr. Buell Gallagher, an old-time and old-method man of good will. Copeland, a former army captain, had maintained peace and order on campus by ruling with an iron-handed, no-nonsense approach. Since he knew who the faculty troublemakers were, having been at the college and active in its affairs for forty years, he acted appropriately, but seemingly harshly, thereby making many enemies who were strongly enough entrenched to influence the presidential-search committee, which deliberately avoided choosing anyone of the Copeland or Hayakawa* type. They apparently wanted someone who, they hoped, would pacify all parties concerned. The illogic of their expectations never occurred to them.

During Copeland's short year in office, he made many changes, not the least of which was the promotion of many deserving scholars who had run afoul of the radical contingent and thus, because of purely political considerations, had been denied their rightful advancement. Likewise Copeland had moved to get rid of some faculty members, who, at the very least, had encouraged the militants to employ violent tactics and, it was suspected but was more difficult

*Dr. Samuel Ichiye Hayakawa, already a world renowned author and specialist in semantics, had achieved international fame of a different kind when he took over as president of strife-torn San Francisco State College, which for close to three years had been a battleground of rioting, arson, bombing, assault, deliberate destruction, and malicious damage. By reason of his particular profession—semantics—he had never been deceived by the stated pretexts for the violence; hence, unlike so many other administrators, he acted forcefully and effectively. Within a short time—long enough for a number of confrontations to reveal that he could not be intimidated and that he would in no way seek to appease or buy off the revolutionaries, the campus returned to academic rather than revolutionary activity. Needless to say, among radical and far-left liberal contingents, his name became a byword for repression, although the effectiveness of his seemingly harsh methods (i.e., his insistence that the students and faculty had to adhere to the rules of behavior that normally govern civilized people) were incontrovertible. At the City College of New York, no sooner did Dr. Gallagher resign, than one department chairman rose to insist that the clergyman's replacement must *not* be anyone like Dr. Hayakawa.

to prove, had also probably helped to plan the insurrections. Copeland's own assessment, before he finished his administrative term, was that he had made many mistakes he regretted. Yet to those who were not strongly committed to radical politicizing of the college, the net balance of his decisions was salutary. He had taken over in the midst of violence and had brought peace, albeit an uneasy one, to the campus. The few attempts at reinitiating trouble had been suppressed before they had had a chance to escalate.

According to various surmises, which may or may not be correct, when Dr. Marshak came in, he received his briefing from those committed to change. Consequently the new president took a dim view of some of Copeland's decisions, and, in effect, acted on occasion to undo what his predecessor had done. He also had the rather naive view typical among many liberal academics that all he really had to do to win the trust and assistance of all dissenting groups was to demonstrate his very genuine good will and his desire and intent to please. This assumption is totally unrealistic in today's crisis atmosphere. The point that has had to be repeatedly hammered home to a great many administrators is that at least some disruptions do not arise because of injustice, sluggishness, or inequity in the "system." They arise from the desire to disrupt. The goals of these disruptions vary. Some are most certainly the work of anarchists and/or Communists who deliberately organize with the intent of destroying American morale. Others relate to almost trivial personal goals. For example, two City College students described to me a conversation which they had had with another student—the leader of one "minority" faction on campus. According to their report, this individual, who was receiving financial assistance to help him pursue his studies, was at the time of their conversation well along the path to failure in all of his courses at the college. The probable consequence of such failure was likely to be an invitation to leave the school. To stave off his own personal disaster he was planning a general strike—the pretext yet to be decided—designed to close down the entire college. He planned to keep the college closed long enough to bring about a repetition of the marking policy of the previous spring. On that occasion a succession of strikes and moratoria differing in stated goals from day to day and even, in a few instances, from hour to hour, had so disrupted the term's work that very few classes, if any, had completed the normally required work for the semester. Consequently, after much heated debate at various policy levels, the teaching staff had been directed to fail no one at all provided that there had been even a remote possibility that the students in question might have raised their marks to passing if they had had the opportunity to take the work of the last third of the semester. The fact that many students had already richly earned their *Fs* was put aside on the humanitarian ground that they might somehow have changed their record but for the disruption and closure of the college. Needless to say, this policy was the salvation of many "students" who had no business being in college at all. Thus, such pupils—some of whom may never have actually attended class at all, quite apart from the additional time lost during the strike—received passing grades without penalty just by virtue of their *enrollment.* Indeed, a few of them, undoubtedly, may not even have attended their own registration but, instead, may well have sent others in to sign up for their courses for them, and so they had no personal experience with the educational institution at all, save for their participation in the activities which had closed it down and prevented others from going through the learning process.

Furthermore, the faculty had thus been asked—or, more accurately, been told—to certify that students had mastered subjects which they had not really had a chance to master. Clearly, of course, not all students had been responsible for the disruptions, and, just as clearly, it was unfair to penalize them for what had not been their fault. Yet the consequences of the humanitarian policy adopted may not always have been fair even to these innocent victims of the disorders.

To take one example, not at the undergraduate but at the graduate level, a *doctoral* candidate presented herself in one of my courses. The woman was a brilliant pupil, and the record showed that she had already taken various graduate courses. She possessed a master's degree. Consequently I quite reasonably assumed that the woman could be expected to know the material fundamental to her master's-level course work. When the student failed to grasp the rather elementary concepts of the doctoral-level course she had enrolled for, some searching inquiry soon revealed that the reason for her apparent inability to understand the lectures was the fact that I had used examples which *anyone*—absolutely anyone—who had completed the master's level course work should have had as part of his proper background. Yet the facts attested on her graduate record were false, not through the woman's dishonesty—she was scrupulously honest—but because her final term had been one of disruptions and her teachers had assigned her course grades based on her having taken only part of the work. She had never actually finished the regular work for the term. The letter grades listed on her record did not differentiate between courses taken and completed and those taken but not actually completed. The master's degree which she held thereby represented a consolation prize. She did not actually know what a holder of a master's degree in her field was expected to know. Fortunately in this instance, the graduate course for which she had signed up had a small enrollment, and, having uncovered her problem, I was able to guide her to the appropriate reading, thus enabling her to make up her deficiencies and grasp the material of the more advanced course. Nevertheless, the seemingly humanitarian policy which had given her grades for work she had not mastered was fraudulent in conception, and it had almost destroyed a brilliant pupil and scholar. How much more likelihood was there that such a policy could harm less well endowed students at a lower level of attainment?

To get back to the problem of the "student leader" then, he was planning to initiate a closedown of the college to solve his own immediate predicament. Clearly the pretext he would have to use would not be that *he* was failing his courses. He would charge ethnic discrimination or military-connected research by faculty members or the war in Southeast Asia or some other "relevant" complaint. In light of the true reason for the planned disruption, as opposed to the stipulated reason—whatever it might be—what *real* chance would Dr. Marshak have to satisfy the protestors? It would hardly matter what explanations he might offer or what administrative actions he might take—short of arresting any demonstraters, that is. The real cause of the demonstration would be unrelated to the stipulated cause, hence not really accessible to anyone taking the demonstration in good faith.

In one report to the Faculty Senate, Dr. Marshak pointed out that he had tried to show one group of demonstrators that he *had* acted in their behalf and that he *had* tried to give them what they wanted, but that they consistently—and persistently—had misrepresented his statements and deliberately denied the good will of his actions. He reported the facts in an aggrieved, incredulous tone of voice that suggested that even when *he* himself was reporting these facts *he* disbelieved. He simply couldn't comprehend why his willingness to do the right thing—i.e., concede almost anything to militants which they demanded—was not enough to satisfy them. He failed to differentiate between pretext and reality. The demonstrators—in this instance the Puerto Rican Student Union—had even reported via the gullible (or sometimes dishonest) student press the details of an alleged encounter between their members and a senior professor in the Department of Romance Languages. According to their allegations, this professor had been abusive, overbearing, and insulting to them. Only one thing was wrong with these charges: the professor in question had not even been on campus at the time of the supposed encounter; he had been elsewhere, and, fortunately, he was able to prove it. In this particular instance, the patent evidence of the dishonesty of the disrupters plus the stature of the professor accused prevented the administrator from trampling the rights of a faculty member. Yet this group was the same one which had caused trouble for two historians (with the consequent resignation of one—Professor Stoetzer, as already discussed) and for one Romance language specialist (likewise mentioned). In the latter instance, it was the faculty member who was dealt with, not the "students." Not until examples, such as the verbal attack on Professor Sas (the senior Romance language scholar), actually occur can the administrator of the Marshak or Perkins type begin to accept the duplicity of the disrupters. Even then such administrators prefer to appease, although no appeasement whatsoever can terminate the disruption, which, as suggested, stems from different motives.

In a similar fashion, Columbia University, beset by disasters through no genuine fault of its own, called upon Dr. McGill, a psychologist-turned-administrator from a California institution, to direct its destiny. Here too the search committee wanted an appeaser rather than a strong anti-militant militant, one who would act promptly and without compunction to arrest and punish lawbreakers. McGill's rhetoric stressed the need for dynamic approaches to confrontation and the importance of grasping the justifiable aspirations of dissenters. His philosophy appeared fundamentally similar to that of Marshak and others sympathetically inclined.

It took several encounters before McGill publicly acknowledged the essential dishonesty of the disrupters. One group, claiming a legitimate "need" for a recreation room, poured hot coffee over the hand of a woman employee of Columbia so as to force her to give them the key. Somehow this sadistic and unnecessary act managed to anger McGill, whereas the preceding steps—such as those which merely involved the "trashing" of seminar rooms, the destruction of property, vital records, and research—never disturbed him enough to get him to act for the rights of *non*disrupters. This time he called on the Faculty Senate to *speak* to the need for firm measures in dealing with violence.

In his own way Dr. McGill was realistic, but only in regard to sensible fiscal measures. The various disorders at the university—from the first insurrection of 1966, led by Mark Rudd, down to the most recent—had cost Columbia untold millions of dollars, not just as the replacement costs for the actual destruction of property, but as a result of increased costs of insurance, increased costs of private police protection, and, more notably, the decrease of contributions from alumni, who rightfully disagreed with appeasement policies and viewed their potential gifts as just so much money down the drain.

Columbia *had* to a large measure been destroyed by the deliberate intent of the original SDS group that had initiated the first disruptions. Famous faculty resigned, retired, moved elsewhere, or, in a few sad instances, died. No one, of course, can unquestionably prove that the deaths resulted from the hostilities in the sense that the victims were shot or physically injured by direct violence. Yet some heart attacks, cerebral hemorrhages, and other causes of "nonviolent" demise undoubtedly stemmed from the aggravation and frustration which so-called cloistered ivy-tower academics had not been able to handle.

As news of the disruptions became widespread, enrollment at Columbia dropped—both in consequence of the fear of violence itself and, of perhaps greater import, as the recognition of the lessening stature of the faculty became apparent. One major graduate department, that of English and Comparative Literature, once world famous, declined and, as a direct result, now has fewer students than it once had illustrious faculty. In one area a replacement professor was appointed who was not even a specialist in the subject he was assigned to teach. Privately, an incoming chairman spoke of phasing out that subject altogether because of the realities of economics.

Dr. McGill, to be sure, was the inheritor of the desperate situation, not the cause. He came into a crisis situation, with the once-great university deeply in debt and sinking fast. Thus he recognized the need to "trim" the budget and to economize in every feasible way. He did this by dropping entire programs (e.g., the theater arts), by tighter control of faculty salaries (thus precluding the hiring of eminent scholars to replace those lost), and by cutting out luxury courses which could not be justified financially. Of course some of these cuts helped signal to observers that the university no longer deserved to hold the first-level reputation it had previously enjoyed, and so many ambitious students, looking to their own future reputations, applied elsewhere, with the consequent vicious downward cycling of reputation and reality.

One point was missed, namely that the choice of appeasement versus nonappeasement of militants plays a central role in determining the outcome of the survival struggle in a *number* of ways, not just in the limited fashion envisioned by the "liberal" administrator. Although capitulation to demands may serve in the short-run sequence to head off some trouble, in the long run it makes clear that the administration acts from fear rather than principle. Occasionally, even if the demands *are* just and even if the administration *does* act from principle, the net impression that results, unfortunately, is still that of simple, fear-based capitulation to intimidation. This point is one that was made eminently clear at confrontation after confrontation at various colleges of the City University of New York. The chancellor, deputy chancellor, and other administrators have repeatedly emphasized the justness, the humane spirit, and the lofty ideals inherent in the open-admissions policy, but militant beneficiaries of that magnanimous policy have just as regularly pointed to the fact that the Board of Higher Education had failed to see this noble ideal until buildings were burned and the individual board members, not to mention administrators and faculty, had been threatened with death. Thus one consequence of doing the right thing under conditions of duress is a disbelief in the motivation, coupled with the view that if violence worked before it will work again. Thus "doing the right thing" under such circumstances is an open invitation to future lawlessness (e.g., the violent takeover of a room for recreation, alluded to, together with the physical measures employed).

A second reflex of fear-based capitulation—sometimes even *pre*-capitulation, the attempt to give what one expects to be demanded—is an alienation of both alumni (with the consequent drop in contributions) and potential students. Once an institution starts to lose current students (one of its economic bases) and to alienate its former students (another such base), it is facing both fiscal disaster and either academic demise or, perhaps worse yet, academic mediocrity.

The irony of the current situation is that those individuals who occupy a middle ground are too often persuaded to entrust their institution to the rhetoricians whose stance suggests (1) that the disrupters have valid cases and (2) that they themselves empathize with, and, therefore, can handle these would-be lawbreakers. In a famous dialogue, Plato once pointed out that the ability to govern well does not necessarily imply an ability to get oneself appointed to the governing post. All too frequently, the clear-thinking of those who see the absolute necessity for strict maintenance of law and order is negated by the misguided liberalism of those who speak of human values, but ignore the values of those campus residents whose ethics include some consideration for their neighbors. Therefore many modern administrators have to be educated on the job, so to speak, although such education (e.g., McGill's, first in California, then at Columbia) entails endless substantive damage to the institutions entrusted to them. In the end they arrive at the very position held by those whose "repressive" policies they once assailed. Even so, some administrators learn, but unfortunately do not have the guts to face the implications of their lessons. Thus, for example, Dr. Robert Goheen, the President of Princeton University, resigned his post after seeing his institution (1) wracked by radical disorders, (2) politicized to a degree that seriously interfered with real scholarship, and (3) become so hostile to dissenting viewpoints (i.e., dissenting with the viewpoints of those at Princeton) that students and faculty would actually deny freedom of speech to their opponents. What is ludicrous is his assertion that in times of stress college presidents *should* not serve more than ten or fifteen years. It would have been more accurate to acknowledge that in times of stress, such as the current era, the type of administrators of the Goheen, Gallagher, or Perkins type *cannot* last even two years.

Few human beings can endure permanently in a post of constant crisis. Indeed, as clearly seen, many cannot endure even short-term hostility. Yet the modern academic administrator must realize that no matter how talented he may be, no matter how skillful or just or wise the decisions he will make, he will still be attacked, if not by one faction, then by another. Consequently if he accepts in advance this unfortunate fact, he may be more inclined to take the long-range view and to preclude future demonstrations by not rewarding current disruptions. He must have the fortitude to make the decision that will benefit the institution on a sounder basis than just the avoidance of an immediate unpleasant confrontation.

Most of all, the modern administrator must have the perspicuity to separate real causes from pretexts. When there are genuine issues, apart from the made-up excuses, he must have a mechanism *already* operative for handling them. Then he can point to his actions as a consequence of such decision-making mechanisms, not as choices dictated from fear. Likewise he must reasonably separate those causes which are within the proper province of his institution from those which are not. A student who wishes to protest poverty in central Africa may have a valid cause, but this cause, noble as it may be, is not properly tied to preventing fellow students from learning physics or chemistry.

7. The Administrative Failure of Nerve: Violence as Expression

As indicated, early expressions of the assault on academia took the form of protests against specific—presumably—*academic* grievances: a supposedly biased professor, the encroachment of a gymnasium on an alleged neighborhood playground (mugger's paradise), the need for recreational facilities, the desire for ethnic equality in education, and so on. Although, as suggested, these claims were only pretexts for the real intent—the destruction of our education institutions—nevertheless they bore at least an outward semblance of plausibility. Innocent bystanders, lacking any overall perspective, could readily accept the complaints as genuine expressions of concern about the issues raised. These same spectators, of course, might also wonder at the speed with which such simple-to-handle problems escalated into major confrontations and at the violence—"guerrilla warfare" would be a better description—that ensued.

Even when the invasion of Cambodia produced a nationwide series of attacks on ROTC property on various campuses, these attacks were seen as "relevant." Yet toward the end of April, 1972, after news of the bombing of North Vietnam had become known, once again protests erupted. However, these protests as carried out at university campuses in different parts of the nation did not—*originally*—aim at the particular source of irritation or even at some outward symbol of that source (e.g., the ROTC). They aimed at simple publicity (beyond the ever-present goal of many disaffected "students"—the excitement implicit in illegal, often violent activities). Disaffected groups seized buildings and made speeches inciting to antigovernmental activity, usually with the assistance of expensive amplifying equipment that regularly appeared in the possession of revolution-minded students; they also carried out various degrees of "trashing." Not all of these activities took place exclusively on campuses, to be sure; bricks crashed through the windows of some banks and local businesses as well. All of this activity fits under the well articulated and often repeated Communist master plan of sowing internal disorder so as to confuse and harass the target enemy, in this instance the American people. Needless to say, much of the violence consisted of the sporadic, perhaps impulse-of-the-moment, kind, as carried out by individuals—usually so-called students.

The activity on campus, however, was far more extensive and well planned. For example, at Columbia University a crowd of about two hundred and fifty gathered at Wollman Auditorium to hear a speech by Rennie Davis, one of the Chicago-7 defendants, who flew in specifically to stir up and thus help enlarge the antiwar response already set in motion by the seizure of a number of buildings and the shutting down, with the consent of President McGill, of the entire university for one day, and of that part which had been seized for several days thereafter.

The point that is repeatedly missed in the confusion of so many disruptions is the organizational planning behind them. Loudspeaker equipment does not just happen to be on the premises when revolutionists need it. It is arranged for in advance. Outside agitators do not just happen to be on campus: they travel there by reason of advance planning. In the earlier days of the disruptions, many of these professional agitators were unknown to the public at large, hence they could be thought of as just members of the local group of protestors. National, even international, publicity, however, has made many of them well known, as witness the Chicago 7, who have been observed prior to and during many disturbances throughout the country. Remember that Jerry Rubin's appearance immediately preceded the Kent State violence, as the presence of other hard-core revolutionists preceded other—perhaps less spectacular—occurrences. In the instance of the April disruptions at Columbia University, Rennie Davis came in after the fact to try to keep the protest going since the student body at Columbia was simply apathetic, more interested in finishing the term's work than in the antiwar agitation.

Three facts are particularly striking about the Columbia protest:

(1) The "protesters" did not try to justify the attempt (largely successful) to close Columbia University down until *after* the initial disruptive activity had already taken place. Only then did the radical group accuse certain Columbia faculty of war-connected research. One professor confronted the students and asked why they had not asked him in advance of the sit-in whether, in fact, he was doing such work for the government. The answer, of course, was obvious, namely that the accusation, as usual, was merely the pretext; the real reason was quite different. The scholar then denied the trumped-up allegation. Other pretexts were later found (e.g., the university owned stock in corporations that did business with South Africa). Early in the seizure, some students reportedly expressed their intent to close Columbia down until the Vietnamese conflict should come to a complete end. How the Columbia University officials could bring about this goal remained indeterminate. Needless to say, even the shutdown of a few weeks, not to say months, might suffice to destroy the university completely.

(2) Much of the active participation in the troubles came from outside agitators. Quite apart from Rennie Davis, who only entered the picture later, one group—that which occupied the Pupin Physics buildings—consisted of protesters described as "young faculty members from other colleges." One was Jay Schulman, a sociology professor suspected by many of having played an instigational role in the take over of South Campus at City College, an institution which had finally arranged to end his contract after long and costly legal maneuvering, starting first with a nonrenewal of his appointment on the

grounds of questionable scholarship but ending in an agreement to permit him to stay in the classroom for one more year, then to pay him a salary for research for another, after which he would depart. I had debated with Schulman on television years earlier, and once asked him what his own specialty was in the field of sociology. "Changing social systems," had been Schulman's reply.

Not all of the dissenters were non-Columbia people, such as the former City College professor. There were local sources of disruption as well, but one should recognize a striking dichotomy in the Columbia group, which fit into two well marked, different classes, a fact recognized by some news reporters. One group was well organized and purposeful, thoroughly conversant with their goals and responsibilities; whereas the other was undirected and less forceful. The latter one may assume were the followers, the hangers-on, always ready to be stirred up. The former, however, did not have the appearance of merely responding to the events of the day. Their coordination suggested pre-planning, not spontaneous activity.

(3) Possibly *the* most salient fact in the disorders was the moral cowardice of the administration. Dr. McGill acknowledged that "most people on the campus . . . (were) anxious to go to class, and most faculty members . . . to give instruction." He recognized that only a relatively small minority of actual Columbia people were impeding the normal activities, possibly about 150 students out of the 15,000 that constitutes the total student body—in other words, approximately one percent. Yet Dr. McGill called in the outside police only after scuffles had taken place between the university's security forces and disruptive or unruly students. Then, when the city law enforcement officers had responded directly and appropriately to the throwing of stones, bottles, and other missiles, Dr. MGill became frightened and ordered the police to leave. Why "students" should be exempt from the normal rules of civilized behavior (which, one would think does *not* normally include physical assaults on the police) he never explained. Dr. McGill asserted that his position of inaction (i.e., of not using the police to remove the disrupters from the buildings so that the normal work of the university could

continue) had the support of those whom he had consulted.*

One may, of course, feel sorry for Dr. McGill, since, as pointed out elsewhere in this book, he was in a situation where no action he could take would meet with universal approval. Yet lack of action was just as positive a response as action. Dr. McGill was violating the rights of those students—who, one should recall constituted the great majority—who wanted to go on with their studies. Eventually an irate group of students threatened to take Dr. McGill to court to force him to fulfill his function of keeping the university operating. This group included many who agreed with the ostensible political goals of ending the war and ending racism in South Africa. Such students, however, failed to agree that depriving *them* of *their* education would bring about the stipulated aims.

The situation seen here of a weak and vacillating administration paralyzed by fear was not an isolated instance. The same failure of nerve has already been alluded to in the discussion of the City College events. The same failure occurred at Cornell and elsewhere. What the administrators continuously fail to face up to is the fact that since *no* action they take (or fail to take) can please everyone, they might as well perform their primary responsibility, namely, that of keeping their institutions operating. All too often they neglect their responsibilities to the main body of students and faculty because of their terror of a vociferous and lawless minority. As seen, sometimes this minority includes outsiders who have no legal justification for their presence at all. When such outsiders bring the institutions to a halt and induce violence and destruction, they should be prosecuted promptly and vigorously with all of the power the academic administrations can bring to bear. Surely such administrators owe no special consideration to those who are not properly part of their jurisdiction at all. Only fear—naked fear—accounts for the refusal to act that has characterized so many academic officials under pressure.

*The fact that Dr. McGill would do nothing was predictable: he had been chosen precisely because of his approach to the handling of such crises. Indeed, in an article that had appeared in the October 6, 1970, issue of *National Review* (page 1052), Jeffrey Hart had already written, "Everyone I talked to was delighted that 'Bill McGill' has now left La Jolla to take over as president of Columbia. On the other hand, they wish Columbia lots of luck. McGill will fiddle while the buildings burn."

8. The Consequences of Capitulation Under Force

As seen, various administrators have—seemingly—chosen the path of least resistance and have tried to mollify out-and-out revolutionists in a never-ending stream of demands that are escalated until the college official is peremptorily told to end a war in some other part of the world or to eliminate disease or racism or "capitalist imperialism," and so on. Some of the stipulated goals (i.e., the elimination of war or disease, etc.) are, to be sure, highly desirable but are far from the capability of any school administrator *as a school administrator* to fulfill. Indeed, they may be well beyond the capability of any small group to encompass, even if one were to take such demands seriously. Other demands (e.g., the elimination of "capitalist imperialism") rest on figments of the demanders' imagination or on the Communist propaganda some of the dissenters take as their bible.

A reasonable response to reasonable requests, of course, should not—and must not—rest on the use of force or intimidation since it sets dangerous precedents. For example, after seeing capitulation after capitulation to threats—disguised, to be sure, as good will and the desire to do the right thing (evoked by the threat of violence)—some Asian students at the City College of New York, normally one of the most peaceful of the minority groups on campus, *correctly* recognized violence as the only direct path to administrative action. Prior to this time, the group had been so law-abiding that many years had passed before any sort of Asian Studies program had been even considered for the curriculum. Not until Black Studies had been tentatively approved, in the wake of violence, had it become possible to induce a recalcitrant administration to allow the comparable ethnic program for orientals. The students, however, had preferences as to who should direct the program. Consequently, when they disapproved of the administration's choice, they seized the office and staged a sit-in which lasted several days, threatening to stay there—or even to escalate the troublemaking—until their choice for chairman received approval.

The newly appointed head resigned, and, after due consideration of the scholarly and administrative record, the president of the college, with the advice of a consulting committee, did appoint the students' choice. When questioned in the Faculty Senate as to whether he had appointed Dr. Tong because the latter was the best man for the job or merely because he wished to pacify the students, Dr. Marshak hesitated a moment, temporized for a few seconds, then said, "Well—all things considered—Dr. Tong is the best candidate available."

I have had occasion to observe the new chairman, who is amiable, well organized, and clearly not disposed to make any trouble himself. According to a qualified source other than that of the college's president, Dr. Tong *is* highly capable, and does represent an excellent choice. Yet one wonders about the question directed to Dr. Marshak. Was the decision one of expediency or of choice? In this particular instance, the students may well have backed a fine scholar. Yet, more to the point, why had a previously quiet and most nonmilitant group of students resorted to illegal tactics—risking jail records—to get their way? Clearly the answer lies in the precedents already given to them. *The only way to achieve results is by force.*

Even if, as well may be, Dr. Tong is the best "available" candidate and even if his appointment should enhance the program, future groups of students now will believe—and will have every reason to believe—that the choice came about only through militant, aggressive, and illegal action. One may ask, then, how will such a consideration sway their future course and choice of action? The answer, of course, is obvious. *Every capitulation—or even seeming capitulation—has a cumulative effect that may lead to more violent responses, even by those who normally would never resort to such tactics.* The real problem lies less in the violence than in the vacillating or weak administrative action that serves as a stimulus to more violence. It might be added that in the attempt to at least lessen the impression of capitulation to force, I related to the Faculty Senate (and to any student observers present) the report about Dr. Tong's excellent capabilities. The damage of another dangerous precedent had already been inflicted, however; one could only reduce the impact, not eliminate it.

9. Undergraduate Entrance Requirements

The major academic resistance to an open-admissions policy at City University rested on the fear that inadequate implementation of what was clearly a political, not an educational, decision would lead to a decline of standards. When, in the aftermath of violence and intimidation, various proposals for instituting a negative quota system to admit larger numbers of academically deficient minority groups were rejected, the Board of Higher Education cut the Gordian's knot by decreeing that *anyone* who had received a diploma from a New York City high school would have to be accepted by at least some division of the City University. How the university would carry out its educational mission was left undefined. The city itself was teetering on the brink of bankruptcy, space for new buildings was lacking (aside from the need for time to build them), and the faculty was totally inadequate as it then stood. Where the new teachers would come from was glossed over by an administrative decision to use graduate students to do for poorly prepared students in college what well trained teachers could not do for them in high school.

Henry Hillson, the principal of Midwood High School in Brooklyn (one of the better schools) and director of the Upward-Bound Program to prepare disadvantaged youngsters for college, pointed out that many city high schools were already graduating pupils with a reading level of fourth or fifth grade in *elementary,* not high, school. Hillson further pointed out that the open-admissions setup would remove any incentive for his students to work hard. The teachers could no longer hold out the promise of college as a reward for diligence and industry: the youngsters would *know* that they were going to be accepted even if they were totally illiterate.

City University officials went about, visiting group after group of concerned citizens, assuring them that standards *would* be kept high —that all of the Cassandras who were predicting doom either didn't know what they were talking about or that they were biased against the minority groups and didn't *want* open admissions to work. While statements of this sort were being made (with varying degrees of sophistication), the City College Curriculum and Teaching Committee was meeting to consider ratification of the following belatedly recognized *fait accompli.* Prior to open admissions, the college had had certain hard-core minimal standards for entrance, requirements of a certain amount of mathematics, foreign languages, and so on. Yet some of the city's high schools were graduating students grossly deficient in these subjects. The committee then was asked to decide whether or not to require that a liberal-arts major (who would have to be accepted regardless of his inadequate background) would be allowed to graduate without *any* mathematics at all or if the college should demand that he must master intermediate algebra before *receiving* a City College degree: prior to open admissions, the students had had to know at least this much mathematics just to get into the college; they then continued their studies from there. Under the *more* demanding of the two proposed alternatives, the new *terminal* point was the same as the old starting point. If this proposal were accepted (and it was), the City College degree would mean no more than what a diploma from a good high school once used to mean, and, in fact, it well might mean less.

I disagreed with the Dean of the College of Liberal Arts and Science: the two alternatives—lowered standards versus no standards at all—were certainly *not* the only options open. However, it was said that the chill which greeted this protest was used to cool the administration building all summer long. Few faculty members even dared to protest the various makeshift expedients that accompanied the changes. Those who did were attacked as a "conservative and unpopular faction who opposed open admissions." Implicit in the accusation was a tacit but clearcut implication of bias against minority groups. Hence many honest educators who could normally have been expected to react sharply to the false promises contained in the offering of an education which was *not* in fact a genuine education remained silent for fear of being labeled "bigots."*

*See Appendix I for the text of a memorandum distributed to the City College Faculty Council, and Appendix II for a memorandum distributed to the Committee on Curriculum and Teaching.

10. Graduate Entrance Requirements

"What difference does it make," said some, "if we admit poorly prepared students, as long as we don't allow them to graduate without measuring up to the high standards of the college?"

The answers to this question were many and varied, and generally pointed to the destruction of the system or, at the least, to a monstrous fraud being perpetrated on a trusting citizenry. Yet politically the idea of taking substandard students and by some still-to-be-worked-out process of turning them into *genuine* college graduates was both challenging and exciting. Implicit in the assumption was the *maintenance* of high achievement levels. The public-relations job was magnificent.

On November 23, 1970, with the first term of undergraduate open admissions not yet half over, the Graduate Studies Committee met. The returns on the enormous gamble were not in, but Dean Zeichner requested the formation of a subcommittee to consider the impact of open admissions on entrance requirements for graduate school. The dean was already on a national committee convened to consider the same question.

There was some discussion of competing devices for disguising the consequences of what was happening. Someone finally said, "After all, what difference does it make if we admit poorly prepared students as long as we don't allow them to take a graduate degree without measuring up to our standards."

11. Student Control

Some of the positions now regarded as absurd cause astonishment to the onlooker who sees only the most recent phase of an insidious and gradual development that underwent several stages before becoming critical. On November 21, 1970, newspapers throughout the country carried the startling announcement that the faculty at Hunter College of the City University of New York had actually voted to give students a say in the hiring and firing of faculty. Similar decisions had already been made elsewhere throughout the country, and others have been made since then. It is, of course, patent that students do have a direct and vital stake in the educational process. It is not quite so evident, however, that students have the technical ability, the perspective, or the competence to direct the course of that education. A later section of this book will deal with the problem of students' ability to judge faculty—a *sine qua non,* obviously, of the hiring and firing process. Here it may be instructive first to document a typical illustration of the step-by-step acquisition of power. Although at City College, from which *this* example is taken, the final right—that of hiring and firing of faculty—has not yet been granted, nevertheless, the process itself, still underway at that institution, deserves critical attention.

In the fall semester of 1967 some students at City College requested the right merely to observe the activities of the Committee on Curriculum and Teaching. Some members of the committee were less than enthusiastic over the idea of being on constant public display, and thus subject to potential criticism, but others, including myself, felt that they had—or should have—nothing to hide and that the experience of seeing the inner workings of the college could be useful to the observers. Two very practical matters, however, dictated the nature of the permission to be granted:

(1) The committee regularly met in the President's Conference Room of the Administration Building. Since the oblong table allowed just a limited number of seats, only a few students could be accommodated, lest the members of the committee have to stand during their deliberations. The intent here was to avoid any disruption of the orderly procedures of the college while still granting nondisruptive rights to the students.

(2) To avoid argumentation and debate over which students were to be assigned the available seats, the committee decreed that the decision would be granted to the Student Senate. Thus, in due course, three students, neatly dressed and on their best behavior, quietly entered the chamber and took their places.

Midway through the term, the students requested permission to talk at the meetings. As one boy expressed the issue, "It's frustrating to sit here and not be able to say anything." Some faculty members felt that it couldn't hurt to hear the student point of view and that it might even be useful to hear from those on the other end of the academic transaction. In any event the committee would not have to follow the students' views if that course seemed unsound. The students, therefore, received the right to participate in the discussions.

One student member was also an editor of one of the school papers. The first time a vote went contrary to his expressed view, a militant editorial appeared with enormous headlines denouncing the committee as reactionary and naming names. Since by then the students, headed by a bearded young man who was now on the committee, were conducting teacher evaluation polls, adverse publicity could hurt a faculty member's rating. Within a sort time, a subtle change became evident: some of the committee's faculty regularly waited to be certain of the student view before *daring* to vote on any issue. Others, of course, still voted as their consciences dictated.

The next step was already foreseeable. It came in the fall of 1968. "What good is participating if we can't vote?" came the complaint. This time those faculty members who were aware of the direct influence wielded by the students merely as a result of their presence resisted the new demand. Those particular faculty members most afraid of being denounced by the students—and, therefore, really the only ones who would be influenced by the students, regardless of the issues—were by the very reason of that fear unlikely to deny the students the right to vote. Thus, the students acquired voting membership on the committee. Regardless of the high-toned statements made about the sharing of responsibility with the students, the latter received the right to vote on the Curriculum and Teaching Committee by virtue of faculty cowardice and self-seeking opportunism, not because it was considered advisable to give them the right.

Efforts were made periodically to increase the number of students on the committee. This move failed repeatedly for strictly mechanical reasons. No faculty member was ready to give up his own seat so as to allow a student to join the group. The seating arrangements, as indicated before, permitted no expansion. Not all committees fared as well. The Graduate English Committee voted to give students parity—as many students as faculty members. In actual fact, this latter vote actually gave the graduate students better than parity since one or another of the professors in the group is normally on sabbatical leave. Incidentally, as soon as the graduate English students received voting control of their committee, they voted to abolish the regular graduate examination. They substituted a two-question simplified quiz in place of the ten-question type which once had covered the entire range of English studies. Overtly, of course, the members of the English Department spoke of progressive innovation. Behind the scenes, however, they deprecated the loss of all standards—and the fact that they themselves no longer had the power to raise the level anymore.

At one of the last meetings for the spring term of 1970 the students on the Curriculum and Teaching Committee lamented that the committee work was arduous and time consuming; it detracted from their regular schoolwork. Therefore they moved that they be granted academic credit for all committee work. Thus they wouldn't have to do as much outside work—this outside work being what once had constituted the normal course of studies. I pointed out that if the resolution were passed as proposed, an entering student, who might perhaps even be illiterate since the college now was committed to accepting *all* high school graduates under the open-admissions plan, could get himself appointed to a variety of committees in his first term. Then, having received academic credit for this committee work, he could soon graduate just by virtue of having told the faculty how to run the college *even though he himself may never have taken a single college course.* The committee passed an amended version of the resolution. The details of the acrimonious debate regarding the justification for giving *academic* credit for nonacademic work need not be pursued here. I noted that, by the reasoning given, if one granted academic credit for public service, the members of the Sanitation Department should all be awarded degrees *cum laude.* If the students claimed that they should get credit by virtue of what they learned in the committee work, by the same reasoning they should also get credit just for what they learned in their travels to get to school:

4 credits for geography (they use the subways);

4 credits for sanitary engineering and/or ecology (they see the pollution);

4 credits for advertising art (they read the signs); and so on.

It took only a few minutes to map out 128 credits for simply being alive—enough for a City College degree. The committee passed an amended resolution (restricting the number of credits allowable for committee work and delaying the initiation of this accreditation until the student members of this committee should graduate, since their altruistic motives in presenting the motion were suspect). Fortunately the Faculty Council rejected the proposal completely, when it was passed on to that group. A slightly revised version of the same motion, however, was introduced—and passed—the following term.

The reason for considering the minor details of the growing transfer of control is the need to see how a valid purpose can be transformed into something not intended. Underlying the gradual shift is the raw fact of faculty cowardice. This cowardice is sometimes physical, sometimes moral, and the latter may shade into opportunism, as when professors seek popularity by championing causes they themselves deplore and know will benefit no one, not even the particular groups they purport to serve. There is an unfortunate fiction that college professors operate only from the highest motivations, that they are not influenced by the stress and turbulence of political events. How far from being true this view is may be seen in the impassioned remark of the chairman of one committee, when, following a particularly frightening outburst of violence on campus, the committee faced the choice of making a decision either on genuine academic grounds or else on the basis of placating threatening militants: "Gentlemen, we're sitting on a volcano. I don't know how you're going to vote, but I know how I intend to." This concerned professor actually forgot even to ask for any possible negative votes on the proposal, so intent was he on avoiding trouble.

12. Student Evaluation

Two simple examples of real occurrences may bring into perspective the problem of student evaluation of faculty. The first took place at a New Year's party. The guests were enjoying themselves. By and large, they had already satisfied themselves on the refreshments, and now they had started to split off into little groups, some to discuss politics, others to chat about old times, their children's latest accomplishments, and so on. One member of the party, an economist, was a graduate of City College. When he met a City College faculty member at the gathering, he eagerly inquired about the institution and about his own former teachers. He particularly wanted to know about Professor Joseph Taffet, of the Economics Department. "You know," he said, "when I was an undergraduate, I never appreciated that man. Yet, when I got to graduate school years later, I first began to realize what a damned good teacher he was. Because of the background he provided for me, I had a distinct edge over my classmates."

The second example concerns Professor S, of the Chemistry Department at a leading institution. Professor S is a raconteur who can keep his audience enthralled indefinitely. His sense of humor always has some unexpected twist. At the first meeting of one committee, when each of the new members was giving his own name and background by way of getting to know each other, Professor S without batting an eyelash introduced himself by the name of the neighbor sitting to his left, gave a succinct but accurate resume to go with that name, then sat down, to the great amusement of those committeemen who actually knew who he was. His neighbor nearly fell out of his chair, but recovered in time to reciprocate by introducing himself as Professor S. The latter, although the very antithesis of the pompous, pretentious college professor, is one of the world's foremost scholars in his field. He also has written one of the most widely used textbooks on his subject. Yet the first time the students decided to compile a handbook evaluating the faculty, they put Professor S's name on the list of teachers *to be avoided.*

Although Professor S can be interesting and charming, he insists that the students be accurate when describing a scientific experiment. He is an exacting taskmaster with precise standards. The negative evaluation and associated humiliation of this great scholar was predicated on the judgment of just *twelve* students out of the thousands he had taught during his entire gifted career. Furthermore, not one entry in the evaluation suggested what marks these twelve had received. One might suspect that at least certain lazy or incompetent students who had richly earned a low grade could wish to use the evaluation as a means of retaliation, regardless of the excellence of the instruction. Other professors of high academic accomplishment likewise appeared on the same avoidance list—a compilation which the chairmen of some departments used as a guide to promotion and tenure.

Both of these examples cast doubt on the competence of students to rate a professor. If, as is likely, some of the students are enrolled in the courses against their own interests or inclinations, whether to acquire a degree as a passport to business or social success or, until the change in the law, merely to dodge the draft, their only measure may be the entertainment value of the course rather than its educational purpose. Not that entertainment is necessarily excluded from the classroom, but some topics don't lend themselves to simple popularization. Furthermore, as the first example shows, students sometimes do not acquire perspective regarding the real competence of their teachers until years after they have left an institution. This observation assumes, of course, that the students do an *honest* evaluation. In some instances, as suggested, the evaluation may degenerate into a popularity contest rather than a serious and useful appraisal. What is worse, on at least some occasions, the teachers themselves —apprehensive about their ratings, which may well determine their professional future—may adjust the courses to a level geared to elicit approval rather than to bring about real learning. In such a situation, the genuine, dedicated teacher is penalized.

13. ROTC on Campus

One of the prime targets of "student" militancy has been the ROTC program. At one rally held at Columbia University in the Spring of 1970, William Kunstler, attorney of the Chicago 7 and, according to some reports, a self-avowed enemy of the American form of government, urged the crowd to do something about the military-industrial complex. He himself performed no physical act that was illegal, but after his speech a hostile crowd marched from Columbia the mile and a half northward, up to the campus of the City College. There, in a frenzy of destruction, they burned the ROTC headquarters, demolished the uniforms, weapons, and other equipment and, but for the intervention of armed guards, might have burned down the rest of the college.

Some "students" were identified and arrested. They demanded amnesty. The treatment accorded them is irrelevant, but the reasoning or its lack that motivated them calls for consideration. Obviously emotions run high with regard to any reference to military service or to the training for that service. Furthermore, many genuine students, fearful either of losing a year or two of their lives, or, worse yet, of losing their very lives to an unpopular war, require little more than a reminder of the potentiality of their being drafted to stir them up. Skillful rhetoricians like Kunstler, aided and abetted by small groups of activists impelled by a variety of motivations, easily arouse mobs to commit unlawful acts. This situation raises a number of discrete issues, among them the following:

(1) whether or not anyone breaking the law—committing arson, vandalism, malicious damage, robbery, assault and battery, even murder—should be immune to the lawful consequences of his unlawful acts merely because he is enrolled in an institution of learning;

(2) whether or not ROTC belongs on campus at all;

(3) whether or not ROTC, or "military science," which it teaches, if allowed on campus, is properly an academic subject deserving of regular college credit; and

(4) what the reasonable limits should be of the relationships between the university, particularly the public supported university, and the government.

A separate chapter will deal with the question of amnesty and, therefore, no further note will be taken of it here. Regarding questions 2 to 4, the following questions and observations may put the problem into perspective.

Should we abolish or retain our armed forces? Obviously, if we plan to abolish them, we will have to rely upon would-be aggressors to be on their best behavior and not to invade the United States. This question framed in this way seems almost asinine, yet there *are* those who would disband our only means of defense. There are also those who hope for a Communist victory in Vietnam and elsewhere. Whether or not the consequences of a Communist takeover of this country would produce a situation to the liking of such haters of America is not worth discussing simply because it is clear that few Americans—if they actually would take a moment to reflect on the consequences rather than allow themselves to be swayed by appeals to their emotions—would seriously sanction the dissolution of our army, navy, and air force. Yet if we are not going to disband our armed forces, we do need officers to staff them.

The various professional academies—West Point, Annapolis, etc. —do not now, nor in the foreseeable future will they be able to, produce enough officers for our needs. The main source of these officers then is the ROTC program. For those who belligerently talk about the military mind or the professional military mentality, one might note that the ROTC has been a force offsetting the orientation of the professional military who enter the cadre of officers via the academies. By the ROTC route, those who have no intention of devoting their lives to military service enter the armed services, serve their time, and, usually, get out.

Of more immediate consequences, without ROTC *there could be no armed forces* or, at any rate, the size of those forces would have to be reduced far below the level requisite for national safety. If we are not going to eliminate the armed forces, and, thus, if we agree that we must have the ROTC, we must also see to it that the ROTC program remains effective. Yet if ROTC is taken off the campus, its decline is inevitable and carries with it the imminent demise of the entire country. Therefore it is certain that the ill-considered acts of many faculties in simply abolishing ROTC in the heat of antiwar movements is not merely unpatriotic; it is insane.

The question of granting academic credit for ROTC work must be examined from two different viewpoints. First of all, what are the general criteria for receipt of academic credit? That is, what kinds of courses regularly receive such credit? One finds that the answer ranges across such a varied spectrum of subjects that almost no answer makes sense or can be considered definitive. Courses from the ethnography of the African dance to Ping-Pong, from ecological perspective to nuclear physics all appear on the curriculum of one or more institutions. Surely some ROTC courses—such, for example, as military history—deserve no less credit than economic or social history. Others such as military marching and drill deserve no less credit than basketball or badminton—both regularly listed as physical education courses.

The motivation of those who suddenly discovered that ROTC courses were nonacademic in nature must be suspect. Why did they not discover the same facts prior to the antiwar movement? The answer, of course, is obvious.

The ROTC program has also provided a means by which many a poor or middle-class boy, who could not otherwise afford to go to college, has received scholarship assistance. This particular argument for ROTC has less force now, in light of the various open-admissions programs which have come into being since then, but it does have some weight in helping private colleges remain functioning. The fees paid by the government can make the difference between the survival or death of many financially marginal, albeit scholastically sound, private colleges.

The question of the viability of ROTC if allowed on campus *without* credit is not clearly answerable. Certainly the loss of academic credit will cause the program to suffer. How far is less certain. If the damage to the program is sufficient to undercut the national defense needs, some hard soul-searching is in order. There are those who, with valid reasons, argue that there should be *no* governmental control of the institutions of learning at all. Such a view regards the government as a hostile, *1984*-like monstrosity advocating and practicing totalitarian thought control. This view is somewhat innocent and naive. Our government is a republic, answerable ultimately to the people. Yet, even if one conceded the theoretical desirability of abrogating all ties between school and government, one natural limit remains: when the national security is so tied to the educational system (as the defense of this country depends on the effectiveness of the ROTC) that the destruction of the country will follow a severance of the government-school interrelationship, then in self-defense the educational system must allow some departure from its strict hands-off code. Obviously, if no country is left, the school system has no purpose. The case of ROTC *is* one such instance which, if all other arguments were valid, would still demand some cooperation between the colleges and the federal government.

To recapitulate the main points then,

(1) national self interest, which carries with it the very survival of a school system, requires:

(a) the retention of ROTC on campus, with

(b) the retention of college credit for the courses;

(2) such courses are no less deserving of credit than others.

One additional point is deliberately passed over by many opponents of ROTC: no one *has* to take the program. Just because one group does not want to serve its country or because another group wishes the country's demise is no reason to deny those who are willing the right to enter the armed services as officers rather than draftees. Hanoi and other anti-American centers would gladly pay to see the destruction of ROTC and the consequences that would then follow. It is unfortunate that many so-called "American" academics are either so lax in their thinking or so hostile to their own country's needs that they support the movement to abolish ROTC.

In some instances their thinking is clear, but their self-protecting prudence or timidity overrides their patriotism. Thus, at the City College of New York, a special committee set up to study the problem of ROTC reported that the ROTC program had merit and should continue somewhere—but not on City College's campus because the space needs of the institution were becoming serious. Members of the committee actually argued that the college would be doing the ROTC program a favor by ordering it off campus since registration in the program had dropped substantially in the year or so preceding the investigation. Only three members of the Senate spoke in favor of retaining ROTC on campus. The student press, controlled to a great extent by antiwar agitators, reported these faculty members as "strident voices." Only eight voted to retain ROTC as opposed to fifty-four against. One open letter by a faculty member (not in the Senate) to a student paper examined in detail the motives of the Senators and concluded that they had voted the way they had because they were *afraid* that SDS would tear down the ROTC headquarters and, of greater moment to these faculty members, the rest of the college with it. This letter was not allowed to be published, but other, perhaps no less patriotic, members of the faculty expressed the same view. If this assessment is correct—and it seems to me to be—once again sheer physical and moral cowardice governed the faculty's actions. To be sure, a pretext—no space—had been provided to camouflage this cowardice, but no protective coloration can completely hide a policy decision based on fear rather than love of country.

On March 19, 1971, then, an undergraduate newspaper, *The Campus,* bore an enormous headline: "SENATE OUSTS ROTC." On the same page there appeared a picture of the college president over the caption: "President Marshak said he 'heartily endorsed' ROTC's ouster."

14. On Speaking Up in Academia

The American ethos holds "I may disagree with everything you say, but I'll defend to the death your right to say it." Such was the guiding dream of the Founding Fathers of this republic—a noble, far reaching dream, and in principle it is still supposedly a guiding rule throughout this country. Evidently, however, this position is not upheld as desirable by everyone in academia. They who dare to speak even demonstrable and easily documented truths viewed as objectionable in certain circles are subjected to vast, punitive reprisals geared to silence all but those quixotic few who place honesty above their own welfare. Often the statements made in all candor are twisted, turned, and misreported in such ways that the speakers find themselves attacked for supposedly holding positions exactly antithetical to their own. The nature of the repression of freedom of speech on campus—where such freedom should be deemed most sacred—varies in degree of sophistication and subtlety from the crude, almost Gestapo-like efforts seen on some campuses to the most refined, difficult to prove, but nonetheless effective, even terrifying tactics seen elsewhere.

At the low end of the spectrum is an anti-war rally held at Stanford University. According to one campus publication (and later confirmed and elaborated by a government major who graduated soon thereafter), the student body was invited to come up to the microphone one by one and rap about the war, to give its opinions, observations, or insights. *Presumably* the rally was to be an *open* forum with *all* opinions receiving a respectful hearing. So it seemed —as long as the volunteers *complained* about the wickedness and immorality of the United States, of the atrocities committed in its name, of the repressive nature of its society and people. Finally one veteran of Vietnam arose to present the opposite point of view—to say that things weren't like that at all, that our country still deserved some respect. He had barely said a couple of sentences, when his "welcome" evaporated, and those conducting the proceedings tried to tear the microphone from his hands. Since he held his ground and continued—or tried to continue—to speak in this vein, several men tackled him and threw him bodily to the platform to prevent his side of the story from being told. This, then, was "free speech" at Stanford University, one of the great and famous centers of learning, not only in this country but throughout the world. Strikingly enough, none of the newspapers in New York carried any report about the transaction. In this instance the effort to stifle opposing viewpoints took place openly and in full view of hundreds of witnesses. Far more insidious is the attempt to punish and destroy those who have the courage to speak counter to the views that those in power wish to promulgate.

Sometime prior to Thanksgiving Day of 1970, the nationally syndicated columnists Rowland Evans and Robert Novak decided to do a follow-up article about the open-admissions policy at the City University of New York. Accordingly, their secretary phoned or wrote to arrange interviews with a great many faculty and administrators (including the deputy chancellor of the university) whom the writers later met and spoke with in December, on an individual basis. Quite prudently, some scholars declined the invitation, and others requested that they not be quoted by name in the article. The picture which emerged from these interviews and discussions and which appeared soon thereafter in more than two hundred newspapers throughout the country (under different captions) was the following.

CRISIS AT CUNY

Utterly baffled by the profundities of first-year history at City College, a newly enrolled freshman this fall told his professor he simply could not make sense out of the textbook "because too many words are just too long."

Such a heart-rending incident could not have occurred in years past. Such a student would have been academically ineligible for CCNY, the tuition-free college ranking among the nation's best liberal arts schools

Under the new open-admissions policy, however, anybody in the city with a high school diploma can enter City University, a sprawling educational complex of junior and senior colleges (including CCNY) and graduate schools.

Although CUNY's administrators deny it, faculty members complain that the incident of the bewildered freshman is commonplace. Thus, the preliminary estimate of critical faculty members is that the quality of instruction is declining and will continue to decline.

"To be perfectly frank," history Prof. Howard Adelson told us, "there are indications that this college is finished as a learned institution."

The avowed reason for open admissions is that a tax-supported institution must provide service for *all* the city's residents, regardless of qualification. The harshly practical reality, however, is that student radicals at CUNY would have blown the lid off the school if the policy had not been adopted. Moreover, some administrators privately praise the policy for an entirely different reason: taking slum youth off the street.

Thus, two grave questions of public policy are raised at CUNY with applications across the country: Is the enormous expense of higher education the best way to care for semi-literate high school graduates who might otherwise drift into crime? And is the high price of drastically lowered academic standards really necessary to achieve this goal?

The financial cost is staggering. The burden of CUNY's 15,000 extra students under open admissions adds another $20 million to the $320 million annual budget without even providing space for the enlarged enrollment. Soon, the annual cost of CUNY will be $1 billion, to be borne by a society reaching the upper limits of its tax burdens.

But the academic cost is even more disturbing. CUNY administrators stress that unqualified freshmen are given remedial courses in reading and arithmetic. The flaw in the program is that the student receiving remedial reading can also take regular courses in history, science, or economics, drastically impairing the level of instruction.

Certainly, the end is near for CCNY as an "elitist" institution where sons and daughters of the poor could obtain a free education of Ivy League caliber. "I think the conception of academic standards is going to change," CUNY deputy chancellor Seymour Hyman told us.

Indeed, the concept is changing radically right now. The Negro or Puerto Rican youth, given a diploma in New York City high schools without regard to ability to read or write, will not be flunked out automatically at CUNY. An informal arrangement proposes that new students not be flunked out until after 1½ years, giving everybody a two-year free ride.

But worried faculty members fear that the two years may stretch to four, and the CUNY degree will become as meaningless as a New York City high school diploma. Hence, the formulation of classics Prof. Louis Heller: "Open enrollments—a political device for conferring a college degree without giving a college education."

Just how many faculty members agree with Heller is impossible to determine. Critical professors described for us a climate of fear, based on actual death threats to faculty members, professors beaten up in their classrooms in the violent spring of 1969, and a rising tide of student power giving students influence over the professional futures of the faculty. Thus, silence is understandable.

But such absence of criticism cannot deflect national academic attention from what is happening at CUNY and particularly at CCNY. In the months and years ahead the cost to higher education of egalitarianism run wild may be incalculable.

This article appeared at different times in different newspapers. I had met with Robert Novak on December 3, spoken frankly but with scrupulous attention to the accuracy and verifiability of everything discussed, and then gone on about the normal activities of a very busy professor with deadlines and obligations to meet. *The New York Post,* the only New York paper to carry the Evans-Novak column, did not run the article until December 29, 1971, approximately a week to ten days after it had appeared elsewhere. The following day, December 30, a massive "rebuttal" was published in the *Post,* featuring Dr. Seymour Hyman. Subsequently a fuller (ten-and-a-half-page) version of Hyman's reply was published in the *City College Alumnus,* a bulletin that goes out all over the world to graduates of the college.

At the January meeting of the City College Faculty Senate, the chairman of the Executive Committee of the Senate introduced a censure resolution on behalf of that committee condemning Professor Howard Adelson (chairman of the City College Department of History) and myself—the only two faculty members who had been quoted by name in the article. I was not present because of illness. Likewise Professor Adelson missed the beginning of the "trial" because of the press of his official duties, not knowing that his lifetime reputation for integrity was up for public discussion. Neither faculty member had been informed of the intent of the Executive Committee. Fortunately Professor Adelson got to the meeting when the acrimonious debate was underway, one in which Professor Arrowsmith compared the proceedings to the Reichstag trials.

Friends telephoned to inform me, then in bed with a raging fever, of the trial and consequences. As soon as illness permitted, the "accused" arranged to speak to the next meeting of the Senate on a point of personal privilege. The text of that reply follows.

Statement by Professor L. G. Heller to the Faculty Senate on a Point of Personal Privilege

At the January 14 meeting of the Faculty Senate Professor Arthur Bierman, acting on behalf of the Executive Committee, offered a motion of censure directed against Professor Howard Adelson and me. I was very sick that day with an ailment from which I have still not fully recovered and, consequently, was not present. I understand that Professor Adelson also was absent when the resolution was first proposed, although he did arrive before action was taken on the motion—ultimately a watered-down statement that passed. I had *not* been informed in advance of the intent of the Executive Committee. I was given no chance to defend myself—or to prepare a defense if any was necessary. I utterly reject the statement made just now by Professor Guerriero that the committee simply "forgot" to inform me because of the "press of business." A censure motion is not just another item of ordinary business. It is not merely one more transaction on the agenda. It involves a human being and that person's hard-earned reputation.

In view of the statements made, affirmed, and reaffirmed at the December meeting of the Senate regarding the need to build bridges in the academic community, I find the proceedings rather extraordinary. If my memory serves me correctly, Professor Guerriero was one of those who spoke to this point. Perhaps, however, the Executive Committee's good will extends only to minority-group students and not minority-opinion colleagues. Even so, one would hope for at least the minimal political courtesies from a group acting as self-appointed guardians of public morality. Approximately the same day that the Faculty Senate was conducting a trial in absentia the Supreme Court of this country was reaffirming—in a case that was widely reported—the principle that the accused has the right to receive the specification of the charges and to defend himself. Perhaps the Executive Committee does not agree with this principle.

One does not have to be a specialist in parliamentarian procedures to recognize that the original intent of a tabling motion was to postpone action on a motion until the appropriate time. I have seen members of the Executive Committee utilize tabling as a device not for postponement but for removing from any consideration at all a motion which they disapproved. It would not have been inappropriate last January 14 to table the motion of censure—and even the discussion—until the accused was here to defend himself. But perhaps our Executive Committee finds itself embarrassed by those who are ready, willing, and able to defend themselves.

I find something even more disturbing than both the motion to censure and the deprivation of the minimal right of defense. At least one member of the Executive Committee has known me for about fifteen or sixteen years. If he no longer has my phone number, he or the other members of the committee can get it without difficulty. I *am* listed in the telephone directory. I would hope that uncovering my number would not exceed the investigative powers of such eminent scholars. Not one person called me to check if I had been quoted accurately. For the record, I had been—but they did not know that. They did not even know if they had a *prima facie* case. Furthermore, not one person called to check if the views expressed in the article reflected my own view. After all, I was quoted for exactly fifteen *words* out of a column of about one hundred lines. I gather that many people had been interviewed by the authors, including Deputy Chancellor Seymour Hyman. Did anyone include him in the censure motion? This Senate has censured Chancellor Bowker, so I would assume that even a deputy chancellor is not beyond reproach as well.

According to the minutes of the meeting, the supporters of the resolution denied that it contravened academic freedom: "it would not affect jobs and promotions." I reject their denial. It is true that a censure motion cannot directly deprive one of a job or, by itself, prevent a promotion, but certainly promotion rests at least in part on the overall evaluation of a scholar. I myself am now up for promotion to full professor. At least some of those who will be sitting in on judgment were in the Senate or later heard about the motion. If one single person is thus influenced, all of my scholarly activity—more than eight books published by the end of this year, fifty articles in professional journals, not to mention various publications I don't even list, editorship of two journals, and so on—will have been negated, without even the courtesy of a trial.

Since the Executive Committee did not care to be bothered with uncovering the facts in the case and since I for one do value my own reputation, I therefore would like to provide whatever clarification I can so as to put the article and the circumstances of my own comments into context.

Last November 25 or 26 I received a long-distance telephone call at my home. When I answered, a woman introduced herself as the secretary of Robert Novak. At first I didn't recall who Robert Novak was but she identified him as the writer who collaborates with Evans in a nationally syndicated column. She said that Mr. Novak would like to speak to me about open admissions at City University. I indicated that I had no special inside information beyond that possessed by many teachers at the college, and that there might be others who were better informed. She said that Mr. Novak would be speaking to various people on campus but that he wanted to speak to me also. I agreed to meet him and settled on a mutually convenient time after she told me what days he would be on campus.

At four-thirty, December 3, Mr. Novak arrived at my office in Mott Hall and remained for about an hour and a half. I call your attention to this hour and a half precisely because I was quoted for fifteen words and Professor Adelson for fourteen. Mr. Novak already had interviewed various other people prior to his meeting with me. Consequently he had some very explicit questions which I assume were intended to confirm or refute allegations already made.

He asked if there had been violence on campus. I said that, of course, I had heard the usual rumors of a great many instances but that I would discuss only those examples of which I had direct knowledge. I then mentioned the ones I was able to recall at the moment. If I had known in advance about this question, I could have written a book. I refrained from mentioning incidents which I knew had taken place if I could not recall the precise names and circumstances. I mentioned the assault on Professor Hennion, whose office is just opposite mine. I myself had seen the cuts and bruises and had heard the story directly from him and other members of my department who had been present. I told how Professor Plant had been thrown headfirst down the stairs at the 145th Street subway station. I myself had seen the head wound he had incurred. I took great pains to keep the details of the chronology straight. Mr. Novak was quite helpful in this respect. Apparently, he already had a good picture of what had occurred.

He said that he had been told of death threats. Were they true? Again I said that I would stick to those instances which I knew were true although I had heard reports of other cases. I myself had been threatened several times, the first instance during the confrontation in this building in the Spring of 1969. Professor Susskind was with me, and was similarly threatened. On that occasion, when I reported the threat to Dr. Copeland, he told me that forty-one other threats had been received that day, including threats to his wife. The most recent instance which I mentioned to Mr. Novak was that alluded to a few meetings ago by Professor Morris Silver. The names of eight or nine professors marked out for destruction were posted outside of Wagner Hall last May.* Some of you may recall that Professor Silver asked one member of this Senate why *that* violation of civil rights had not been investigated. My own name was on the list.

Mr. Novak asked me about standards under open enrollments. I replied that it was probably too soon to be certain but the comments of various colleagues who get more entering freshmen than I do—I teach mainly elective courses—suggested a distinct downward trend. I refrained from saying "an appalling downward trend," as had been related to me. I also indicated my view that the actual grades would probably *not* be a valid index since many teachers, being human, would mark the students on the basis of comparison with their fellow students rather than with some absolute measure. Hence an average student by previous standards would become an "A" student since he would then shine by comparison with his nearly illiterate classmates. I also pointed out that many teachers might be influenced by the prospect of student evaluations. Whether student evaluations of teachers are just or not, the teachers' own expectations of what the students may do inevitably must play some role in governing their actions. I pointed out that these observations on standards represented only opinions or hearsay but that there *had* been some concrete and direct results of open admissions on standards and that these were *not* matters of opinion. After the Board of Higher Education had obligated City University to

*The crime for which the militants had wanted to murder the scholars had been the dastardly act of continuing to meet with and teach their classes despite violent attempts to close down the school. When informed about the threat, the author had promptly typed out the following reply and then had posted it next to the original notice:

(1) If teaching classes to those who—unlike you—want to learn makes me a scab, then I am proud to be a scab and will continue to be one.

(2) Since you weren't brave enough to sign your obscene threat, I doubt that you will have the courage to carry it out.

Professor L. G. Heller

accept all high school graduates, it was then realized that some high schools were granting diplomas to students grossly deficient in mathematics, languages, and other subjects. Up to last year a student had had to have advanced algebra to get into City College. If he didn't have it, he might be admitted, but with advanced algebra* as a condition he had to remove. Last May the Curriculum and Teaching Committee was asked to approve either of two possibilities: to allow liberal-arts students to graduate without any requirements at all in mathematics or, alternatively, to require that they take intermediate algebra before college *graduation*. Thus, either way, their terminal point would be lower than the old pre-open admissions starting point used to be.

Some members of the English Department have argued that liberal-arts majors don't really need mathematics. I disagree but am willing to discuss the point on its own merits. However, anyone who claims that the decision to drop the math requirement was a purely academic decision is a liar. It very well may be that eventually the requirements would have been dropped even if there had been no open admissions. That view is clearly speculative. It is not speculative to assert that the action that *was* taken to drop the requirement arose from a *fait accompli*, not from a scholarly judgment.

Mr. Novak asked me if I was *for* or *against* open admissions. I suspect that my answer may surprise some of my colleagues: I said that I was *for* open admissions—but only if it represented a genuine, properly implemented program, not a fraudulent labeling of a political act. My views on open admissions are a matter of public record, but I find myself amazed at how often views which are diametrically opposed to those I hold are attributed to me. Some of you may recall a number of discussions and debates I had on television and radio. If so, you may remember that I advocated open admissions long before the Board of Higher Education did—at a time, in fact, when a committee was still seeking a legal formula for a negative quota system, in the name of minority rights. I was not unaware of the need to help underprepared students. (You will note that I don't say *minorities* or *majorities:* I say merely students who needed assistance.) Years earlier I had discussed with Dr. Buell Gallagher the type of courses that might enable such students (regardless of the cause of their deficiency) to get a *genuine* education. I did not—and I do not—believe that merely putting students lacking certain basic tool skills into a regular classroom will help them. It can only convince them that they are incapable. It can also lower the achievement level of the entire class. However, I do not want to use the

*I should have said "intermediate," not "advanced" algebra, but the point being made would not have been affected by the difference. Indeed, if anything, the distinction merely emphasizes the low level of standards.

right of personal privilege to expound my educational philosophy. I allude to these facts here only because I feel that part of the intent of the censure motion arises from feeling—inaccurate as is it—that not only have Professor Adelson and I opposed open admissions but that we do not *want* open admissions to succeed. This view is wrong on two counts, but the allegation *was* made in the *New York Post* on December 30. If I had not been sick, I would have replied appropriately then. To be sure, this charge was not made by the Executive Committee of the Faculty Senate, but since it arises from the same circumstances—including the Evans-Novak article that upset the committee—it is necessary to comment on it here.

Professor Adelson and I had also advocated a preparatory program, via the University Centers for Rational Alternatives, prior to the open-admissions policy. You will note that Professor Adelson never said that he *wants* standards to drop. Quite the contrary, he is chairman of a committee designed to monitor standards. He merely expressed his opinion regarding the reality of what *had* been taking place—at least as he saw it. I assume a member of the faculty is still entitled to have an opinion, regardless of whether or not it agrees with that held by his colleagues.

I myself was asked by Mr. Novak what *I* thought the future held for City College. I also expressed some pessimism for the immediate future but, in regard to the long-term view, indicated that the college is a public institution, that eventually reappraisals would take place and that reforms would be brought about. I indicated my hope that *eventually*—I didn't know when—standards would be raised again.

It happens that I have a commitment to City College which I think goes beyond that of many of my colleagues. It is certainly not simply a daily job I perform in return for wages. I was an undergraduate here. I met my wife in a classroom less than one hundred feet from where I now stand. My older son is a student here.

I have always been proud of the City College principle of free tuition and high achievement, and have been proud to teach here. Consequently, although I have occasionally received offers to go elsewhere with advantages in both pay and rank, I have never even considered them—or, for that matter, even mentioned them by way of seeking academic advantage, though I have taught at a number of other institutions, both in this country and abroad, as a guest lecturer.

However, let us reconsider the basis of the censure motion.

Is it the mention of violence? There *was* violence, and continues to be. Note the events of this very day on which Dr. Marshak could not get to the Senate meeting because of the seizure of a building by a militant student group. But I refer you also to various appraisals already on record, made by different graduate departments at the college. *They* complain of the violence and of the effect which this violence has had on the recruiting of teachers and students. Some of these reports antedate the Evans-Novak article. Since *they* have taken official note of it, should *I* reply to a direct question that I am afraid to answer the query for fear that the Senate will censure me?

Is the basis the mention of threats? There *were* threats.

Is it standards? I clearly separated opinions from facts.

I don't think telling the truth is necessarily a disservice to the college. The facts are exactly what they are. I *do* think that evasion or lies would not be in the interest of City College. *I* can appreciate City College with all of its defects—and I see them without diminution or magnification.

If you don't like the facts, change the conditions causing them: Upgrade the standards! Upgrade the services! But don't downgrade the truth—or freedom of speech.

February 18, 1971

The reception to the reply was striking. Colleagues who had ceased speaking to me suddenly became friendly once again. The chairmen of five different departments and two deans went out of their way to indicate their approval. The wife of one colleague sent a note indicating her satisfaction, and lamenting that she had not been present in person to hear the rebuttal. Being a shrewd political analyst, however, she questioned whether any of the members of the Executive Committee itself had actually been influenced. She was undoubtedly right in her appraisal. More went on behind the scene than was immediately apparent on the surface. The ordeal was not over. My reputation was not yet out of jeopardy.

The City College Alumnus is a little staple-bound, soft-cover publication of thirty-two pages that is put out presumably by the Alumni Association but is actually edited by the college's Department of Public Relations. It goes out by the tens of thousands to the homes or offices of CCNY graduates and faculty throughout the world, carrying news of college doings, chitchat about faculty, alumni, and students, and serves to keep these groups informed about the alma mater.

The issue that went out in March focused on the controversy provoked by the Evans-Novak article. The first article discussed the column as "a blunderbuss article on the City University's open admissions policy," by implication an assault on the integrity of the college and a fallacious misrepresentation of the true state of affairs. The *Alumnus* reprinted the entire text of the article—a page and a half in the bulletin's format. What followed, however, was a ten-and-a-half-page "letter" by Dr. Seymour Hyman, the Deputy Chancellor of the University. The contents of the letter indicated that copies had gone out to *every* newspaper in the country. Hyman, who, as indicated, had been quoted by the columnists as saying "I think the conception of academic standards is going to change," took upon himself the task of correcting the misrepresentations. His "open letter" was headed "CUNY replies . . . "

It must be pointed out that parts of this letter had already been quoted by the *New York Post* on December 30, 1970, the very day following the appearance of the Evans-Novak column, a fact suggesting that the *Post* had already submitted the text of the article to the CUNY administration long before the day on which it appeared. Hyman, it must be surmised, also had utilized the vast resources of the university to prepare his reply, since he apparently had tracked down the specific circumstances alluded to in parts of the column and even had a complete breakdown of the students in my classes. He had drawn the wrong inferences and had misrepresented part of the facts, but the very circumstance of his having these facts indicates the network of resources at the Deputy Chancellor's disposal.

Before commenting on Hyman's reply, further perspective on the subtle propaganda that was being spread may be seen in two observations. One involves an additional inclusion in the issue. The other involves a seemingly accidental omission.

(1) Immediately following the text of Hyman's letter was a little one-paragraph note indicating that Arthur Bierman had been named Acting Associate Provost. Bierman, it must be borne in mind, was the chairman of the Executive Committee of the Senate which had initiated the move to censure Professor Adelson and myself. Thus, by a seemingly unrelated and innocuous news release placed in the appropriate place, one of those attacking Adelson and Heller was being subtly praised. The details of the paragraph suggested the great

things being accomplished by Professor—now Provost—Bierman.

(2) The omission is all the more striking. At the end of the issue, in a section entitled "in the world of BOOKS," a regular feature of the journal, the *Alumnus* reported the publication of eight volumes written by graduates of the college and two by faculty members. Brief descriptions of the books followed most of the listings. I had also had a book published in the time period since the preceding issue of the *Alumnus*. The editor-in-chief of the bulletin had not only known in advance of the imminence of that publication, but had requested—and received—a copy from me. The merits of a volume play no role in any decision to announce publication. If that assertion were to be made, one could point to some of the enthusiastic responses which greeted the appearance of *Toward a Structural Theory of Literary Analysis*—among others one by the Pulitzer-Prize winner, Professor Mark Van Doren, surely one of the most eminent and respected literary critics in the world, whose praise of the book will be deleted here for modesty's sake. The omission of the merest mention of the book in *The City College Alumnus* must be seen as part of a deliberate slanting of the issue to downgrade the reputation of those purportedly attacking the views held by those in control of the university, and to upgrade the reputation of those supporting those views and policies. Needless to say, when it was suggested that this slanting had taken place, elaborate explanations for the omission were forthcoming. The facts, however, speak for themselves.

More disturbing than the slanting is the fact that Dr. Hyman's letter actually contains a direct attack, both individual and collective, on Adelson and Heller. The editor-in-chief of the publication did not (1) inform the accused of the attack which by virtue of publication seemingly acquires official sanction—as though the very fact of who wrote it were not adequate, and (2) did not offer space in the publication for a reply if any were deemed appropriate. Thus a publication with public backing was being utilized as an instrument of official vengeance.

Despite any potential reply privileges in some *later* issue of the magazine—more will be said of this point after the discussion of the letter itself—the reputations of the accused professors would suffer in the time-span between issues and the professors would, in all probability, not even be able to reach the same audience to undo the damage to their reputations—since even if they receive all issues, many individuals don't read *all* issues or don't read all issues in their entirety.

Returning then to Hyman's letter, the Deputy Chancellor suggested that Dr. Adelson "teaches one graduate course" and that thus his experience with open-admissions freshmen was "nil." The reference to "one graduate course," it may be surmised, was designed to suggest an image of a lazy department chairman far removed from the actual educational transaction and thus not really qualified to say anything at all regarding the open-admissions or any other program. In actual fact Professor Adelson regularly teaches a full and heavy load *in addition to* his administrative work. The kindest view would be that Dr. Hyman simply had his facts wrong. A less kind view would suggest that he was deliberately misrepresenting the facts. Furthermore Adelson had never suggested that his statements were predicated on direct experience with the students. However, as chairman of the Department of History as well as in his capacity of unofficial clearing house for all the cross-discussions and gossip about what transpires at the college, Adelson was fully aware of the experiences of his colleagues and of their views, which his comments reflected. Many of these faculty members were afraid to state their views publicly.

In referring to myself, Hyman asserted the same charge as that directed against Adelson: "Professor Heller has about as much classroom experience with OAP freshmen as his colleague, Professor Adelson." He then went on to point out that only eleven freshmen were enrolled in the "one undergraduate course (given by Heller) in which freshmen can be enrolled." The very fact of Dr. Hyman's having such prompt access to this information suggests the organizational setup backing him. I, who taught this course, had never prior to Hyman's charge actually bothered to note which of the students had entered via the new open-admissions policy and which via the normal means: such a dichotomy was irrelevant once the students were already in the classroom. Preferential handling of one student as compared with the treatment accorded another represented a philosophy repugnant to anyone who believes in democracy and impartiality (not, of course, indifference).

Hyman then argued that "every one had a high school grade average above pre-OAP criteria for City College admission." He did not, however, bother to give the actual averages although the same organizational resources which told him of the eleven freshmen could just as readily have gathered *this* evidence, which would have been more meaningful than his unsupported surmise. He said he "would be very surprised" if these eleven lacked the "ability to read and write."

Although, as indicated, I had taken no note of my students' classification before or while teaching them, some investigation seemed in order in light of Hyman's charges. A quick check revealed two things:

(1) Of the *eleven* freshmen only *one* was an entering freshman—hence a potential OAP student, since the Fall semester had been the first under open-admissions.

(2) A penciled notation appeared in my record book next to the name of the *only entering* (not upper) freshman, hence the only student who conceivably might have been an open-admissions pupil. The boy's midterm mark had been 20 percent out of a possible 100 percent, and the notation read: "virtually illiterate."

Thus Dr. Hyman had gotten facts which were presented as evidence, but they were both inaccurate and misleading. The readers of the *Alumnus* could not have known these facts, though.

The determination of the administration to discredit the opposition may be seen both in the substance and the rhetoric of the accusations. Reversing the true facts, Dr. Hyman asserted that Heller had "inveighed against implementation of open-admissions" in the "public testimony of 1969." Apparently those who agree with Dr. Hyman "speak," or "assert," or "explain." Those who disagree "inveigh." A slightly different slanting had actually taken place in the *New York Times* article which had directly reported the Joint Legislative Hearings alluded to by Dr. Hyman. On that occasion, when I had raised questions for consideration which were intended not as opposition to open-admissions but rather as necessary obstacles to be dealt with *if* open admissions were to have a genuine chance of being successful, the New York newspaper did not really misstate anything. Yet somehow the speaker who followed me on the witness stand was *Dr.* Kugler. The speaker who preceded likewise had a doctoral title. Yet the report of the paper omitted the doctoral title when referring to Heller, despite my possession not only of one Ph.D. degree but of course work to the *post*-doctoral level in each of three separate fields. Likewise, the article did not refer to me as "Professor," a title which it could have used if there had been any doubt about the doctoral label. This subtle slanting—"inveighed" rather than "argued," and the omission of prestige-bearing references—characterizes the treatment accorded opponents.

More serious, of course, than the slanting was the mendacious claim that Adelson and Heller had *opposed* open-admissions—and the correlated insinuation that they didn't *want* it to succeed. Thus Dr. Hyman could charge "a good case of the self-fulfilling prophesy distorting reality." As indicated in the reply to the Faculty Senate, neither of us had opposed open admissions. Both of us had, in fact, suggested such a policy. The testimony referred to by the Deputy Chancellor—a cause for great agitation at the time—had indicated that certain very specific kinds of implementation were necessary if the policy were to be a serious academic endeavor and not a political expedient for disposing of troublesome militants—a revolving-door policy, in effect. In the analysis I presented, the question of financing was an important consideration. I asked where the money would come from—apparently a very embarassing question which no polite scholar should have asked. I also pointed out that if open-admissions were passed and if no funds were then appropriated to accommodate the increased demands, the *lack* of money could be—and probably would be—used as a pretext for abolishing both the *free* open-admissions policy itself and, worse yet, the free-tuition policy of City University, which had been staunchly defended since the college had been founded more than a century earlier. This free-tuition policy had provided countless youths from poor homes with entry to a world that would otherwise have been forever closed to them. Out of the ranks of the tuition-exempt scholars had come Nobel Prize winners, statesmen, judges, scientists, leaders of every sort. The repayment to the city in terms of money via higher salaries, which were taxable, had been more than satisfactory by fiscal measures, but the repayment in terms of their accomplishments transcends any measure. This consideration and others of similar nature had prompted my questions.

At the present moment New York City is in desperate financial trouble—a situation I predicted—and there is serious talk of completely abolishing free tuition at CUNY. Yet if this free-tuition policy is destroyed, where does that leave the open-admissions dream? Perhaps Dr. Hyman will now charge the two professors with undermining New York City's financial structure all by themselves (via a self-fulfilling prophesy?). Indeed, almost every point I raised has proven accurate. It has been a constant source of amazement how the administrators who attacked those of us raising such points seem continually surprised that self-evident problems should come home to roost. Doubtless they imagine some dark conspiracy against the forces of light and justice and compassion for minority groups. Yet who is hurt most by the abolition of free tuition, the rich or the poor?

The major point to be grasped here, of course, is the unprincipled means employed to crush "opponents" or to destroy their reputations. These means vary from sheer overpowering brute force, as seen at Stanford and elsewhere, to the more sophisticated use of communicational media—newspapers, radio, television, and even public-supported magazines or brochures—as at City College. In the latter instance, one irony is the fact that the victim himself helps pay for the means of his torment! Many academics, both faculty and administrators, believe that theirs is the only path to salvation and that they are the sole possessors of the truth. They pay lip service to the principle of free speech, but don't really believe it. Their paranoid views allow no room for legitimate opposition or loyal dissent. Freedom of speech becomes a fiction when it carries massive penalties. Under the current academic setup, freedom of speech means only freedom to agree, *not* to disagree.

15. Bending Over Backward to Safeguard the "Rights" of "Students"

Seven times that week telephoned threats to Fairleigh Dickinson University had forced the evacuation of buildings lest someone be killed by bombs reputedly set to go off. Each time members of the local fire department had abruptly dropped what they were doing to speed to the campus in a desperate effort to avert disaster, meanwhile leaving the conflagrations they had been fighting to continue unchecked. The firemen took such menacing calls seriously since just a few days earlier deadly explosives had destroyed a TWA plane. Furthermore, incidents such as the explosion at Ohio State University—which had destroyed the lifetime's work of several scholars and had actually killed one graduate student—were too well known to allow either the academic administrators or the fire fighters time to make leisurely and well justified decisions as to which threats were real and which just an annoying species of harassment. If even one threat out of a hundred should come to fruition, resulting in the death or maiming of students or faculty, the personnel who had been irresponsible enough to disregard the menace could never justify themselves. *All* threats had to be treated as genuine.

Again came the ring of the phone. Again a voice announced the planting of a bomb. The dean was in despair. He hated to disrupt classes for the eighth time that week, yet he dared not allow business as usual. Obviously something would have to be done beyond the wearisome necessity of dealing with the immediacy of this particular threat. Once again the call proved to be an empty one, but shortly thereafter the dean addressed the faculty at a meeting and announced that in the future an effort would be made to track down any person calling in anonymous bomb threats over the phone: arrangements were being implemented to record the voice of the speaker. Perhaps the new science of voice printing already used with great success by special divisions of law enforcement agencies in several parts of this country might prove adequate to the task here.

No sooner had the dean made the announcement than one member of the faculty, who reportedly regarded students as "victims of an exploitive society," expressed her view that to record such conversations would constitute an invasion of the students' privacy. She hoped that they would be informed of their constitutional rights.

The dean replied that they *would* be informed—that their voices were being recorded.

It might prove a point worth pursuing to ask how she knew that the callers had, in actual fact, been students, if she didn't actually know who they really were. More to the point here is the sequel to this unbelievable interchange. One might perhaps expect the academic community to regard a defense of the right to privacy in the commission of a felony as irrational. If so, one would be wrong. This vigilant protector of the right to commit a crime without inconvenience was elected chairman of a Committee on Student Life and Welfare. One might, of course, admire her adherence to the principles of civil rights a bit more if it had been *her* home that had been ablaze when a bomb threat diverted the firemen from their primary job. The fact that one faculty member acted as she did is far less important, perhaps, than the vote of confidence implicit in her election by her colleagues. Unfortunately, the academic community regularly—and repeatedly—acts on oversimplified generalizations (e.g., the catchwords here are "civil rights") and consistently ignores the overall context in which the generalization must be applied. Such a simplistic reaction is tantamount to a rejection of reason itself and is a consequence of mental laziness.

Regretfully the foregoing example is just one out of countless illustrations of the same type of reasoning—one which fails to consider *all* of the facts. I am not unfamiliar with the history of the gradual, painful, millennia-long struggle to achieve the freedom, rights, and protections guaranteed only in this country and in no other nation in all the world. Yet freedom and right are like two-edged swords, requiring prudence and responsibility. An individual's right, no matter how sacrosanct, does not—and should not—include the freedom to harm his neighbor. Threatening phone calls certainly constitute an abuse of "freedom," involving both harassment and the genuine possibility of damage to persons and property. They are *not* the legitimate exercise of a right won at such grave cost through the centuries. To consider them as proper uses of freedom ignores the natural limitations to, and the responsibilities of, freedom. In a like fashion, the student's right to protest whatever it is he disapproves —war, pollution, inadequate recreational facilities, or anything else —has legal and moral boundaries, namely those which involve injury to others or which prevent others from going about *their* self-chosen "right-protected" business. Unfortunately, as indicated here and in other chapters, academia has been so onesidely preoccupied with protecting the dissenter that it has both tolerated and even encouraged the most outrageous violations of the fundamental rules of civilization *while pointedly ignoring the rights of law-abiding members of the community.*

Another, but by no means isolated, example of the foregoing point occurred during the weeks of debate following the takeover of buildings at City College of New York, alluded to earlier. Bending over backward to show their good will, the faculty voted a resolution expressing its sympathy with the goals of those who had occupied buildings and shut down the institution. Yet, when word came that a group of engineering students, desperate over the loss of classes which threatened *their* goals (the Dean of the School of Engineering pointed out that unless the classes resumed immediately, under law, the students would lose credit for the term), were attempting to reopen the North Campus by boldly entering the buildings and ejecting the trespassers, the same faculty voted a motion of censure of such lawlessness. In other words, the faculty, whose principle *raison d'être* is, presumably, the furtherance, not the prevention, of the educational process, had approved or, at least, tacitly accepted the illegal violence aimed at closing the college, but, having themselves prevented the use of police force to reopen the school, had condemned only that violence employed to allow students to continue their education.*

*The determination of some faculty to close down the college became even more apparent later, after the Board of Higher Education had appointed Dr. Joseph Copeland as acting-president *explicitly so that he would keep the institution functioning.* The Faculty Senate voted a resolution calling for Dr. Copeland to issue a directive canceling all classes. He firmly refused. To do otherwise would have been contrary to his own judgment and inclination, not to mention being illegal as well: Mario Procaccino, New York City's Comptroller, and some City College students had taken out injunctions which had resulted in a court order directing the college to open and stay open. Nevertheless, many faculty members vilified the biologist-turned-administrator for his refusal. Again, the Faculty Senate met and reaffirmed the earlier motion, disregarding the crucial fact that Dr. Copeland would have to commit a felony to comply with it. The anger against the acting-president approached the pathological; some faculty and students even went so far as to accuse him of being racist—a charge regularly leveled at anyone not properly appreciative of the demands of the radicals and far-left liberals, and obviously an absurdity. Proof of this point appears in the fact that Dr. Copeland and his wife had adopted a number of children, including one who was black and two who were oriental in background. The Faculty Senate met once more and again voted the resolution. This time Dr. Copeland feared a total split between him and the faculty, if he should still defy them, would render the situation totally untenable. Therefore he executed a legal subterfuge, calling for confrontations between faculty and militants *as an educational experience.* Thus, in compliance with the determined efforts of the Faculty Senate, he did in effect cancel classes, although still maintaining the semblance of legality. Very few faculty attended these meetings. Many who did go in good faith to these "discussions" received threats to kill them if they failed to capitulate to all of the demands. Nonetheless, the militant faculty's efforts to halt the real business of the college had succeeded.

16. The Breakdown of Civil Communication

"Go fuck yourself, you cock-sucking, mother-fucking bastard," snarled the leader of the revolutionists when Dr. Buell Gallagher, the Christian minister serving as president of the college, moved as though to say something. The clergyman sank back into his chair, and the obscene verbal abuse mounted in intensity. Possibly six or seven hundred faculty members—many, scholars of international reputation—sat in stunned silence. Forty or fifty armed militants crowded the steps across the podium, brandishing makeshift weapons—jagged metal bars, clubs, knives, and spears—while the vituperation continued. Behind them towered an enormous, world-famous mural depicting Alma Mater presenting a diploma to a new graduate, who stood clad in cap and gown, as the Muses, and also a solemn assemblage of scholars, scientists, and various other learned men from the past and present watched. This was Great Hall, pressed into service in recent years for registration, but ofttimes the scene of solemn academic ceremony or scholarly activity. From the very same podium senators, governors, mayors, Nobel laureates, Pulitzer Prize winners, philosophers, physicists—distinguished men of every type—had spoken. Now a very belligerent "student" stood there—mouthing obscenities.

According to later reports, this young man had entered the college the preceding September in a special program that paid him fifty dollars a week to attend classes. In his first term he had failed most of his course work, then, in the next (or Spring) term, he hadn't even deigned to go to class since he had been too busy planning revolution; however, he had not neglected to collect his stipend. Now he occupied that venerable and sanctified podium by virtue of his militant group's marching into the hall during a meeting of the entire faculty and shouldering aside Professor Bernard Bellush, the presiding chairman. The young man now could vent all of his buried rage and frustrations in venomous speech. The target of the moment was Dr. Gallagher, but clearly anyone would do, and, indeed, others were soon to receive the blast of his hostility as well as that of other revolutionists. At the moment Dr. Gallagher could suffice as the whipping boy most conveniently at hand to serve as the symbol of "capitalistic imperialistic racist oppression." It did not matter that this particular college president had always been in the vanguard of civil rights advocates or that he had been the very reverse of biased. His courteous and considerate treatment of all who had ever passed his way counted for nothing. By civilized standards, one did not have to admire or even approve Dr. Gallagher's administrative record before according him the minimal social amenities—but Great Hall had abruptly ceased being part of civilization.

After the first shocked surprise, a few—very few—of the faculty rose to call a halt to the outrageous stream of obscene invectives as well as to protest the forcible interruption of the meeting, but Dr. Gallagher waved them back. "It's all right."

A stream of professors hastened their way down the center and side aisles, some frightened to the point of physical illness, others outraged at the proceedings and unwilling to lend the dignity of their presence to the confrontation. Perhaps half remained behind, some curious to find out what the militants had to say, others because they felt that their own presence might be needed to accomplish whatever serious business impended. Still another faction of the faculty fully approved the events, and they sat watching in satisfaction. A few of the last-mentioned group made amused, jesting remarks to their immediate cronies.

Professor H. Park Beck, of the Department of Education, switched on a small transisterized, battery-operated tape recorder, endeavoring to preserve the precise details and tone of the transactions, but the revolutionists wanted no permanent memorial to their actions, whose unseemliness could hardly bear public scrutiny. Several militants converged on the scholar, insistent that he turn it off. He refused despite threats to both his instrument and himself—but his colleagues, after a vote, decided that this demand of the militants should be honored. Other members of the revolutionary band spotted people in the audience whom they denounced as reporters of the local newspapers. These potential witnesses too had to go. The faculty agreed that all of the proceedings must take place behind locked doors with no monitoring at all by the media. Thus the tone was set.

In the weeks and months that followed, the participants in the confrontations—one can hardly honor the interchanges by titles such as "deliberations" or "discussions"—employed language less as a device to convey information for rational consideration than as a bludgeon for purposes of intimidation and assault. Dr. Joseph Copeland, who, as indicated, was later to take over as acting president of the college, served as a member of a three-man team, originally formed for purposes of observation but later used for negotiation, at secret meetings with the leaders of the militants. He has related how the students—if they were students—spent hour after hour, not discussing the demands but simply cursing and reviling Dr. Gallagher, who sat head down throughout the transactions, not replying at all. The clergyman's acceptance of the indignities heaped on him deserves analysis and comment, but more to the point is the obvious fact that if the goal of the belligerents had been the stipulated five demands the so-called negotiators would have bent their efforts to negotiating, not to their vile tour de force in invective and perverted mockery and degrading of the college's chief administrator.

Yet although one can by some stretch of one's mental capacities conceive of this type of action by angry students, one finds it more difficult to grasp the fact that supposedly scholarly faculty members condoned, approved, and even defended this misuse of language and the concomitant breakdown of the minimal requirements for rational discourse. Furthermore, many of them participated in the savage verbal onslaughts on their colleagues, although they did not need to resort to obscenity to achieve the same vicious impact. Nevertheless, some of these faculty members were not above employing such crudities on occasion. Likewise, they did not hesitate to deliberately misrepresent or distort both the intent and meaning of their colleagues. For example, Professor Nathan Süsskind, one of the older and certainly most distinguished members of the faculty—a scholar recognized the world over because of his achievements in his own field of Yiddish lexicography—rose to point out the parallels between what was taking place at City College and what he had witnessed in Germany in the 1930s. He tried to indicate that what they were seeing, however, was *not* just a local disturbance, but that it formed part of a pattern observable elsewhere, and that this cause likewise was the same wherever the pattern occurred. In making his speech, Dr. Süsskind used a phrase which to him and to many others simply meant *and was intended to mean* "Let's talk plainly without any subterfuge." The phrase he used was "Let's call a spade a spade." Professor Alf Conrad, the leader of the faculty group supporting the militants, immediately rose to jeer, "You mean 'Call a nigger a nigger,' don't you?" I, for one, can attest that Professor Süsskind was completely unaware that some people use the word *spade*—from the phrase "black as the ace of spades"—as a scurrilous term of opprobium for black men, since the other use of the word had to be explained to him after he inquired privately what Professor Conrad had been shouting about. It was, of course, clear from the context that Conrad had been fully aware that he was misrepresenting the remarks of Professor Süsskind, who is not at all biased, as Conrad had tried to suggest. Nevertheless, Conrad's jeer got its fill of snickers and catcalls, followed by further mockery from other members of the clique, all at Professor Süsskind's expense.*

*The crudeness and frequency with which some faculty leveled the charge of bigotry at their colleagues, even in the absence of any (to this observer) plausible pretext (other than the scholar's dissent with the position or interest of the accuser) can scarcely be overstated. One faculty member noted privately how at one meeting Professor Beck, one of the more sensible and surely most widely respected members of the staff, pointed out that only one or two years of remedial work would be inadequate to bring poorly prepared students up to the college level. A colleague who was then actually serving as one of the negotiators—supposedly for the faculty, not for the militants (although the results of a week of negotiations consisted of total capitulation, without a single change of any iota of the demands)—said that "those remarks could only be interpreted as implying a genetic inferiority."

Professor Howard Adelson, one of the bravest men on campus, rose in indignation to cry "Shame" upon the faculty and to admonish it for such crude and ungentlemanly behavior. During most of the proceedings, members of SDS roamed the aisles, threatening, intimidating, and lending their voices to the cacophony of booing or cheering, depending upon who the speaker was. The foregoing tactic, that of discrediting the opposition by suggesting that it spoke only from motives of racial or ethnic bias, was employed over and over again with striking impact by the more effective members of the faculty sympathizers. The threat of being labeled a bigot frightened at least some members of the faculty far more than any physical danger ever could have.

The meetings, acrimonious and hostile as they were, did not totally lack for lighter moments. On one occasion, Professor Süsskind, embittered by the unbelievable incivility of his colleagues and outraged at the extraordinary motions they were passing, rose. Stepping up to the microphone, the short, gray-haired scholar uttered, tongue in cheek, one of the most magnificently ironic speeches ever delivered. Professor Süsskind said in effect that the faculty should pass a resolution thanking those who were destroying the college and the American way of life. Of course, he meant the speech to be understood as sarcastic, but his presentation was so subtle—and the anti-law-and-order group so lacking in perspicuity—that many of them were uncertain as to whether or not he really meant his words; others swallowed the comments whole and applauded loudly. After Professor Süsskind had sat down, one enormous, bearded SDS member, carrying a club, went up to him and asked, "Did you really mean it, Professor?"

"You heard what I said, didn't you?" he replied, with a perfectly straight face.

The youth looked at the older scholar in bewilderment, no doubt remembering some of the latter's earlier speeches. He hesitated a moment, then finally said, "Well, keep up the good work, Professor."

Most of the meetings continued in an air of such savage hostility that one waited expectantly for the physical slaughter to begin. One woman on the faculty, appalled at the intensity of the verbal belligerence, proposed four motions to the group, all of them aimed at restoring, if not friendliness, at least the outward appearance of civilized conduct. Her offerings evoked great merriment among the worst of the faculty offenders, who rose, one after another, to amend, change, and otherwise vitiate the first three motions, rendering them innocuous and ineffective.

With a despairing look, Professor Rackow stepped back to the microphone to plead for the passage of the one remaining motion—that forbidding the use of obscene language. Mocking laughter drowned her out.

"What is obscenity?" called one voice.

"Has to lack redeeming special value," snickered another.

Hilarity convulsed the faculty jeering section. The group, however, was unwilling to take even the slightest risk that they or the militant students might have to be civil. Consequently, one instructor interrupted Professor Rackow to ask for the microphone, ostensibly to speak to the issue.

She relinquished it, expecting to move her motion after he had made his observation and after appropriate discussion had taken place.

Instead the young man snapped, "I move to adjourn," not even waiting for her to move away.

"I second the motion," called another voice.

Professor Rackow immediately tried to protest this unscrupulous attempt to prevent a vote on her motion, but, after a brief word regarding precedence under parliamentarian rules—a move to adjourn takes precedence over a regular motion and, furthermore, is not debatable—Professor Bellush called for a show of hands. The motion to adjourn passed, and, thus, Professor Rackow's last try at the restoration of civility failed, never even reaching the dignity of an actual vote. One must stress the fact that this rejection of an attempt to call for civilized behavior was not accomplished over the objections of the faculty: they voted to adjourn; they did not have adjournment imposed on them.

The unseemly conduct and the vulgar and aggressive use of language depicted here was not restricted to the City College campus.

The same scenario was played over and over again wherever violence motivated by the desire to destroy rather than to achieve positive ends erupted, regardless of the surface-level pretexts. At Cornell University a badly shaken faculty abruptly capitulated to all militant demands after previously having firmly resisted them. In an apologia printed in the *New York Times* Professor Milton Konvets explained the craven behavior as a last desperate attempt at restoring the fundamental social contract on which civilization itself rests. Clearly, he and his colleagues had been terrified of a blood bath unless they gave in. Fear of physical violence, of course, could readily have been minimized were it not for the no-police-on-campus syndrome discussed elsewhere in this book. Respectable faculty and administrators, however, should not allow themselves to be bullied, mocked, and intimidated by a presymbolic use of symbolic language. To do so belittles the millennia of development of civilization itself.

At the University of Pennsylvania Professor Henry J. Abraham, the chairman of the University Senate, found himself in disagreement with the President and Provost, who held "to the proverbial position that 'sticks and stones will break your bones, but names will never hurt you,' and that the joys of the open mouth ought to be permitted full rein." As Abraham put it, in a plea for civilized discourse printed in *The Academy,* ". . . the language emanating from some of the students present (at three fora, the last one held February 25, 1972, at College Hall 200)—aided and abetted by a small faculty claque—was more akin to the language of the gutter or, at best, that of a men's locker room, than that of supposedly reasonable and intelligent members of an institution of higher learning . . ." and "to have undergraduates tell members of the faculty to perform certain physically impossible acts upon themselves—is neither humorous, nor Chaucerian, nor should it be permitted to pass in line with the 'sticks and stones' syndrome. No such vulgarisms and insolence must be given a public forum! If individuals wish to address themselves in such fashion in private—that is their privilege. But to provide them with a public forum is not only self-defeating to the principle of rational discourse, it is insulting to the very concept of a forum and is wholly counterproductive of the exchange of ideas among presumably reasonable individuals in a university setting."

Surely *the* major function of any college or university is the free and unintimidated exchange and transmission of information and ideas. Anything at all which impedes this function is inimicable to the very concept of a center of learning. Very obviously the use of scurrilous language and abusive verbal tactics *aims* at nothing but intimidation and harassment. It involves the renunciation of reason as the means for demonstrating the worth of the ideas presented. Although it may serve as an emotional outlet for infantile individuals, such use constitutes either a tacit confession that the perpetrator does not believe that he can convince his audience of the value of his suggestions—instead he must bludgeon the hearer into acceptance, despite disbelief—or a simple act of sadism.

Many academicians—such as the administrators at the University of Pennsylvania, perhaps—do not specify and enforce fundamental rules of conduct not, one may suspect, because they believe that such rules are undesirable but rather because they see certain practical difficulties. For example, in the attempts to prevent the passage of rules for decorum at City College, referred to earlier, certain faculty members raised the problem of a definition of "obscenity." Their intent, to be sure, was simply that of harassment and mockery, but they *were* invoking a very difficult problem. How does one lay down the rules so that they are perfectly clear and understandable, subject to no misinterpretation, distortion, or abuse? Unfortunately those dealing with such riddles often lose sight of one fundamental distinction, that between an explicit readily verifiable definition of a category and the actual existence of the category itself, however recognized, even by *non*-technological means. An analogy may clarify this distinction. Barring pathological complications such as the loss of the sense of taste, anyone who has ever tasted a strawberry recognizes its characteristic flavor and would never confuse it, say, with vanilla or chocolate or lemon. Yet no one has ever succeeded in *defining* the taste of strawberry in a useful way, one subject to the restrictions indicated. Nevertheless one's inability to so define this taste does not and should not prevent the manufacturers of strawberry-flavored gelatine or ice cream from so labeling their products. An excessive preoccupation with verifiable and unambiguous definition would raise the question of how one knows that the gelatine and ice cream are "really" strawberry flavored if one had not defined the phrase *strawberry flavored.* The answer, of course, need not rely on a battery of lexicographers, chemists, physiologists, or psychologists debating the problem: a simple taste test by anyone who had previously internalized the experience of strawberry flavoring would give a definitive result. In a like manner, terms such as *obscenity* can reasonably be left to the "taste test" and should not be allowed to be used as obstacles to the framing of rules for civilized conduct. Obviously there may be marginal cases, just as there may be marginal flavors reminiscent of, but perhaps not quite identical with, the usual notion of strawberry. Where the *intent* of the conduct, verbal or otherwise, is constructive, the administration of any reasonable rules is not difficult. Where the intent is hostile or belligerent, rules may be violated anyway. It is one of the functions of academic administrators to see to it that academia remains a setting conducive to the academic function. Those unwilling to abide by rules geared to this function should be allowed no place at all in any institution of learning, since by their very acts they prove themselves antagonistic to rational discourse. Certainly both students and most assuredly faculty must *never* be allowed unrestrained freedom to abuse and intimidate those who disagree with them. As suggested repeatedly in this book, none of the precious freedoms guaranteed by the United States Constitution was ever intended to include the right to harm someone else. To lump the breakdown of communication indiscriminately under a heading such as "freedom of speech" is a monstrous distortion of the ideas of the founding fathers, one which should not be tolerated.

17. Bias Disguised as Antidiscrimination: The Hiring and Assignment of Faculty

Two particularly pernicious forms of reverse bias in academia deserve special consideration since they both subvert American concepts of equality before the law and also pose grave threats to scholarly standards. The first pretends to defend the rights of minority students and to confer improved educational benefits upon them. The second purports to protect minority scholars from discrimination in hiring and promotion. Directly or indirectly, however, both reflect the same militancy and political opportunism seen elsewhere, which seize upon pretexts and do not truly arise from genuine injustice.

One facet of the former variety of reverse bias appeared in the examples cited earlier of the harassment of two history professors—Professor Stoetzer and his successor in the same department—and Professor Sas of the Department of Romance Languages. Aside from the fraudulent allegations (including the outright lies leveled at Professor Sas, hardly a matter of interpretation since he hadn't even been on campus at the time of the supposed incident), the major fault of all three faculty members seems to have been their extraordinary lack of foresight in not having arranged to be born in Puerto Rico, a deficit which, according to their accusers, permanently incapacitated the men from teaching or dealing with students of Puerto

Rican background and from ever discussing or teaching subjects related to Puerto Rico in any way (i.e., language, history, etc.).

The reaction to the militancy deserves notice. Members of the history department, outraged at the absurd charge that only a Puerto Rican could teach Puerto Rican history, refused to fire a scholar assigned to the course or to appoint a Puerto Rican in his place. They had not reckoned with the administration's determination to pacify all troublemakers. A new Department of Puerto Rican Studies soon came into being, and it proposed to the Curriculum and Teaching Committee a new two-term History of Puerto Rico. By coincidence the teacher assigned to teach the course happened to be Puerto Rican. Presumably he had the proper academic qualifications also, but, barring the remote possibility of gross and overt incompetence, no official inquiry was likely to consider his credentials once the new department had certified him. The administration had not dared to encroach upon the history department's rights by taking away the already extant one-term History of Puerto Rico—the political repercussions of such a high-handed action would have been horrendous—but, instead, it actually condoned (connived at?) a most extraordinary duplication of courses. The justification for adding the new two-term sequence held that the course was more highly specialized than the old one-term program. There is, of course, nothing at all wrong with offering intensive work in some particular area, yet in an undergraduate college where a single course covers all of the Middle Ages in the whole of Europe and where there is a budgetary crisis it would appear to be an extraordinary luxury to have three separate History of Puerto Rico courses on the books, even if one does not count into the reckoning the fact that a separate History of Latin America course also covers the same territory, albeit in a far more abbreviated form. The courses *can* be justified academically, but, just as clearly, they would never have come into being without the violence or the threat of violence.

The allegation that "only a——can teach a ——" (fill in the blanks with identical or semantically related words) is not an isolated happening. In 1969 a number of students at the City College of New York requested that Arabic—a subject not a regular part of the curriculum—be given. Professor Abraham Halkin, a Jewish rabbi teaching in the Department of Classical Languages and Hebrew, and a lifelong student of Arabic civilization and culture, was a highly competent scholar of the Arabic language. Furthermore, he was one of the most famous teachers at the institution, having been mentioned in print with reverence by many of his distinguished students. Professor Halkin decided to offer the course. He would receive no special compensation. This course was a last offering of love by a great scholar near the end of his career—he had taught at the college for forty years—as an accommodation to his students. At the first meeting, a number of Black Muslims appeared, dressed in characteristic Arab garb. When Professor Halkin started to teach, one "student" asserted that the scholar's pronunciation of one word was wrong and that therefore he was unfit to teach the course. The group disrupted the proceedings, refused to let the class continue, and, after the bell rang, crowded into the departmental office where they harassed and frightened the secretary (who incidentally had no authority to remove Professor Halkin from his teaching assignment, even if she had wanted to), with whom they argued in very belligerent tones that "Only an Arab can teach Arabic."

The absurdity of the situation can be apparent perhaps only to someone who knows something about the Arabic language. First of all, Professor Halkin was teaching the highly prestigious classical pronunciation used by well educated Arabs when they recite the Koran. Secondly, pronunciation and other features of Arabic vary extremely widely from one village to another, even when the villages are no more than five miles apart. The student who had, according to one report, "passed through" North Africa, had once heard—briefly—some local (provincial) dialect. The notion that an eminent scholar like Professor Halkin should be judged incompetent on the basis of his pronunciation of a single word and, furthermore, that the assessment of this alleged mispronunciation should rest on the unproven assertion by a beginning student who knew next to no Arabic at all is patently unjust. Nevertheless, the disruption and the attendant unpleasantness continued for some time, embittering the last year of teaching for Dr. Halkin—leaving militancy and hostility as the final memory of an otherwise distinguished career.

Bellicose claims of a like nature, namely that "Only a ——can teach——," occurred and are occurring over and over again both at City College and elsewhere. For example, Professor Louis Amaru, a white scholar teaching at Ulster County Community College near Kingston, New York, had been a pioneer in the field of the history of black people. He had pursued this interest and made himself a specialist in the area long before others—either blacks or whites—had "discovered" the subject, before the study of black history had become "in." When Amaru had begun, there had been no syllabus guides or neatly packaged texts produced to order to meet a growing and highly profitable, albeit worthy, demand. Professor Amaru had been forced to develop his own curriculum in a subject then devoid of guidelines or teaching or learning aids. Because of his consuming interest and dedication, he had blazed his own path, bringing together material, collating, studying, clarifying, achieving perspective and shedding light where there had been darkness and *terra incognita* before. Amaru introduced the fruits of his scholarship into classes at his institution, creating a new course. *Later,* in the wake of various political events, others came to recognize the subject as one worthy of serious consideration. Eventually, however, the study of black history came to be tied to the search for and expression of black identity.

In December of 1970, the Department of History at Wayne State University sponsored a conference on the subject. Many prominent scholars, both white and black, attended this meeting in Detroit. There Professor Amaru was told, overtly and covertly, that "Only a black man can teach black history. . . . The black experience cannot be understood except by a black." Professor Amaru observed, with dismay, the disparagement or rejection of some of the white speakers by virtue of their skin color, not the substance of their scholarship. What was worse, some of the white scholars, placed on the defensive and perhaps feeling subliminally guilty about the black experience in America, not only tolerated but occasionally even said glowing things about the inferior or mediocre work of some of their black colleagues, although there appeared little doubt that they would not have accorded the same courtesy to white colleagues had the latter produced equivalent work.

Professor Amaru was to encounter this attitude—rejection by some (not all) blacks, mainly young militants rather than older scholars, and apologetic acceptance of this chauvinistic view by some whites. Amaru later was to turn down speaking engagements and to suggest instead black scholars for the assignments whenever he anticipated that his audience would be predominantly black. He hoped, thereby, to avoid the unpleasant confrontations he eventually came to expect as a matter of course.

There are two variations to the position being illustrated here. One asserts, in effect, that only an in-group member (black, Puerto Rican, etc.) can comprehend the subject matter properly. The other holds that only an in-group member can emphathize with and understand—and thus properly teach—the in-group student. The former position would have only blacks teaching black history or black literature, regardless of the audience and regardless of the actual competence of white scholars. The *reductio ad absurdum* of this position might be a statement such as "Only a plant can teach botany." Clearly one doesn't have to be a horse to judge a horse race—or a corpse to teach medical students how to conduct an autopsy. Furthermore, this view completely ignores the actual history of scholarship, which contradicts the position that only an in-group member can fathom a subject: it was, for example, Champollion—a Frenchman, *not* an Egyptian—who first deciphered the ancient Egyptian hieroglyphics, building on insights of an English scholar, Thomas Young. It was a German, Heinrich Schliemann, not a native of the territory (now part of Turkey), who so believed in the Homeric description of Troy that he searched for and found that fabled ancient city. Innumerable instances attest the fact that an outsider with enthusiasm, talent, perception, or determination may make major contributions to a field. Should such would-be scholars be barred from participation? Obviously, the only proper qualification for teaching a course is the teacher's knowledge of the relevant subject matter and his ability to communicate that knowledge.

The second position—that only in-group members can teach in-group members—leads to a rather extraordinary set of courses: black mathematics (whatever that may be), Puerto Rican physics, and so forth. Unfortunately, at some institutions there have been attempts to set up such courses in which in-group members teach others of the same in-group. The consequences to standards, needless to say, are devastating. That is, if a university has a scholar of exceptional eminence in a specialty, it cannot assign him to teach his subject if the particular students who enroll for the course do not belong to his ethnic, religious, or chromatic group. Thus the students who are supposedly being protected against racist or other teachers incapable of empathizing with them are also deprived of the privilege of studying with a real master. Instead they must get their instruction from someone of less competence but greater acceptability on the basis of in-group membership.

All of the foregoing examples represented (supposed or fraudulent) attempts to protect students from the effects of bias, with the negative consequences suggested. Equally or even more destructive in potentiality have been the misguided efforts to protect or advance the interests of minority scholars or would-be scholars in academia. One major thrust took its impetus from the Civil Rights Act of 1964 designed to "prohibit discrimination in employment because of race, color, religion, sex, or national origin and to promote the full realization of equal employment opportunity through a positive, continuing program . . ." The intent of Congress had been both commendable and clear. Nevertheless the interpretation and implementation by the Office for Civil Rights of the Department of Health, Education, and Welfare has produced and still is producing the reverse of that intent.

At least a major share of the problem arises from an overly simplistic reliance on statistics, particularly on the type which would compare the percentage of a minority group's distribution in the population as a whole with its percentage of representation in a given occupation. The fact, say, that there are no women playing in the backfield of the Baltimore Colts or no Eskimos represented on the New York Board of Rabbis does not necessarily signify bias on the part of the athletic or religious organization. After all, how many women or Eskimos (a) have qualified for the jobs and, of these, (b) how many have applied? Statistical underrepresentation can stem from any one of four main causes:

(1) genuine bias,

(2) historic patterns of traditions, goals, or aspirations,

(3) trade union practices designed not for discriminatory ends but for the economic protection of the members, and

(4) accidental statistical fluctuations.

When there is real bias underlying the nonhiring of some group, normally there should be more direct evidence beyond the simple statistical measure. All too often people of genuine good will accept the charge of bias as though the mere assertion made the discrimination a fact. Such naivete may itself lead to, rather than prevent, injustice—namely, the injustice perpetrated against the institution or group accused of discriminatory practices. Certainly statistical underrepresentation should rightly evoke inquiries about *why* a minority has not achieved better representation, but it should not by itself be the prime evidence for accepting the charge of discrimination as true. As will be shown after a brief consideration of other (nondiscriminatory) causes of statistical underrepresentation, unfortunately, the direct—and untenable—equation "underrepresentation equals bias" *has* been made, despite evidence that the statistical measure reflects nondiscriminatory practices in many, possibly most (though not necessarily all), academic instances. Furthermore, the steps by certain administrators to remove the alleged discrimination have themselves been instances of genuine and undesirable bias.

A different type of *de facto* underrepresentation of minorities in certain fields is that which arises from the historic patterns of employment traditions and goals. The members of the particular group either strive toward or, alternatively, *avoid* striving toward work in some specific field simply because this area or goal does or does not accord with their aspirations. As has been pointed out elsewhere, the fact that very few blacks or Jews work in the tugboat industry does *not* imply job discrimination: very few members of these groups have ever considered getting jobs in this field. They simply have no traditions which would lead them to seek this kind of position. Probably, for the most part, they haven't rejected the possibility: the thought of trying has never even occurred to them. Whether or not they would be accepted if they were to apply is a different and interesting, but largely irrelevant, question. The problem has never been put to a test. Clearly this kind of statistical picture arises from causes other than simple bias.

Aspirations, of course, may change, and these revised considerations should *eventually* show some statistical reflexes, provided that bias does not in fact exist. Yet one should not be too eager to assume bias even when the mathematical measure does not change promptly since there necessarily are two *phases* in any reorientation of goals. The first occurs when the minority-group members decide to try for a position which they have previously never considered before; the second, when they finally meet the competitive or qualificational levels necessary for employment in the field. For example, most reputable colleges and universities require a doctoral degree as a fundamental and minimal prerequisite for an academic career. Thus, although some statisticians point out that blacks, who constitute ten percent of the entire general population, do not achieve anywhere near that proportion among the faculty of most institutions of higher education, the analysts, either deliberately or naively, ignore both of the central considerations referred to earlier:

(a) How many of the minority-group members have qualified for the jobs?

(b) How many of those who have qualified have also put in their applications for the positions?

Less than one percent (.8 percent according to one study) of the Ph.D's granted in this country have gone to blacks. Thus the total pool of black scholars from whose midst academia *could* properly hire black faculty members without a lowering of the qualification level necessarily constitutes less than the ten percent which the blacks have in the population as a whole. What is more, not all of even this small group have in fact applied for academic positions. If under the present circumstances, the representation of black scholars in academic circles were to reach the ten percent seen in the population as a whole, one could only conclude *then* that bias did exist—against nonblacks—and/or that the educational institutions were lowering their standards and abandoning the merit system so as to reach down (ignoring better qualified scholars) and hire those previously regarded as unqualified.

Before examining in detail the actual responses to statistical measures, one should consider the other bases for underrepresentation. The third variety suggested above—economic protective practices—*can* bring about *de facto* segregation, but it stems from causes other than bias, most normally from the need or desire to preclude an oversupply of workers in a field, a situation fraught with dangerous consequences to the workers thus forced into competition for the limited amount of work.

The control of the labor market by unions is designed to maintain fuller employment possibilities for the select in-group members (chosen by any of a variety of potentially arbitrary standards or criteria). For example, in the field of electronics, one union in the eastern section of the United States rigorously restricted new membership *only* to the children of the then-current members. Hence a father could bring his sons into the fold whenever they qualified in terms of training. Insofar as can be determined, this limitation was not intended to keep out blacks, Puerto Ricans, Orientals, or any other particular minority. It was, as indicated, geared to the protection of the people who already were members. Obviously, since there previously had been very few blacks, Puerto Ricans, and so on in the union, the rule did in effect keep other members of these groups out. Nevertheless the intent had never been discriminatory. Thus, to take one instance, Marvin K's father and uncle both had belonged to the union and, not unreasonably, Marvin himself had anticipated joining at some time in the future. Membership in the union was a virtual necessity if one were to be allowed to work in the field. Unfortunately, Marvin delayed his application a little too long: his father died before he had a chance to vouch for the young man. Hence, although his uncle and, later, his cousins, who were members, were willing not only to recommend Marvin but even to testify that Marvin's father had wanted his boy in the union, the strict regulations forbade any recruitment other than that in the direct father-to-son line. Marvin's application was rejected, and he was forced to leave the city where he had been born and where he had grown up so that he could seek employment in another part of the country where the union rules were less stringent.

One can argue whether or not the foregoing protective practices constitutes discrimination in the broadest sense. Certainly Marvin had not been kept from working in his chosen field because of his color, religion, ethnic origin, or any other cause normally used as a measure of bias. Yet, by and large, the father-to-son limitation did, with occasional anomalies, act selectively against those groups not previously represented in the membership of the union. Hence, after serious disruptions, strikes, and even violence in certain areas, such as Pittsburgh, civil rights activists did get the federal government to use its powers to rectify the situation and to open up specific fields such as the construction industry by virtue of the financial control the government could exert through the awarding of contracts. It is, of course, entirely possible that in some instances the underrepresentation of blacks, Puerto Ricans, and other minority groups actually reflected genuine bias, as well as the economic protectionism which occasionally came to the same end, *although without the same intent.* In any event, the particular circumstances found in the construction industry had made alert observers aware of a new major tool in the civil-rights arsenal—the power of governmental award or deprivation of financial contracts. In the construction industry, of course, the minority groups mentioned had both a strong goal motivation and the technical qualifications. There *were* blacks who possessed competence in carpentry, bricklaying, and the other building trades. Therefore, any contractor who actually wanted to comply with the governmental requirements normally had available an adequate pool of qualified workers from which he could hire minority workers *without lowering his standards of competence.* Undoubtedly, there may have been local exceptions to this generalization (i.e., the possibility that in some limited geographical areas there may not have been enough trained plumbers or electricians among the desired minority group). Such sporadic situations reflected the normal statistical random distribution that is inevitable in a free society where the citizens have the right not only to pursue their own vision of happiness but also to avoid the types of employment they regard as personally uncongenial. For the most part, in the construction industry as a whole such limitation in the minority-group pool of qualified personnel was not the rule. However, many governmental officials and many academic administrators have attacked the problem of underrepresentation of minority groups in the colleges and universities as though it were exactly the same as that which existed in the building industry. No misconception could be farther from the truth, and no single set of administrative decisions based on this misconception could be as disastrous as the "affirmative action" program being forced upon academia from without and within.

One should realize that most institutions of higher learning *must* respond to the ruling of the Department of Health, Education and Welfare (HEW), based as it is, on a misguided statistical measure, since so many of them depend on governmental contracts to keep them solvent. Thus, with numerous colleges and universities barely on the marginal edge of economic survival, the new threat can change or actually destroy virtually the *entire* American higher educational system, by either the direct or the peripheral consequences of the new pressures. HEW, for example, independently notified a number of institutions, Columbia and Cornell among them, of the necessity for immediate compliance with the directive governing minority-group representation on their staffs or else they would face the loss of further governmental support. The responses varied, not only from institution to institution, but even among the different groups within each organization. Numerous behind-the-scene struggles took place with only the results showing. Columbia refused to comply, claiming, undoubtedly justly, that it never had been guilty of bias. In this particular battle, HEW apparently backed down, possibly, one may surmise, because, among other consequences, any protracted and *public* legal battle over the constitutionally questionable action would expose the negative bias inherent in the plan itself. Columbia, however, already in desperate straits financially, had to shore up its public image or face additional violence from the neighborhood groups, enough perhaps to ensure its demise; hence its administrators entered into agreements to participate in various expensive community projects. Whether this decision came about *because* of the public charge of bias, reported in all of the local newspapers, with a consequent exacerbation of any already existing explosive situation, or whether it had been decided earlier to head off the potentially disastrous consequences of local instigation, there can be no doubt that a charge of bias made by an official governmental agency and widely publicized by local newspapers carries infinitely more weight than the same charge made by individual agitators. In any event, Columbia had committed itself to the spending of funds it could not reasonably spare, and thus worsened an already intolerable financial situation. There is, of course, nothing wrong with any organization contributing to local projects. Indeed, such philanthropic activity deserves commendation *provided that the organization can afford the expense.* Columbia, however, is a private, not public institution whose proper mission is—or was—education. Anything that threatens or even detracts from the goal encroaches on the *raison d'être* of the institution. Only time will disclose what role if any, the HEW actions have played in forcing the commitments as one part of a necessary public-relations campaign.

Since the administrators of Columbia refused to accept complacently the naive but damaging statistics-based charge of bias, the potential impact of the HEW order was peripheral rather than direct, although, as indicated, the adverse publicity implicit in any charge at all—"Where there's smoke, there's fire," some will say—contains the seeds of actual catastrophe.* Other institutions responded differently, hence faced, and still face, a direct and far greater threat. At City University of New York, the presidents of the constituent branches and other high administrators met and decided in principle on an "Affirmative Action Plan." The first phase consisted of questionnaires designed to categorize the faculty and students into racial and ethnic groups. The computer print-out on one personnel-inventory form directed the recipient to "Check One" of the following: "Black White Prt.Ric. Orient Am.Ind. OtherSpan. Ital.Am.

*After this book was already in proof, newspapers carried the information that Columbia had capitulated to HEW and was instituting an Affirmative Action Program (i.e., a quota system under a different name, as discussed in the pages which follow).

Other—Specify." Obviously, the basis for the extraordinary grouping rested less on any valid scientific classification than on the current crop of pressure groups demanding increased "rights." Correctly anticipating that many faculty members would be outraged at the notion that skin color, ethnic background, or any other criteria but scholarly merit would play a role in determining appointments and promotions, Dr. Marshak had a note of explanation sent out with the questionnaires. In it, he also indicated that if the faculty failed to fill in the information themselves, it would be filled in by others. Nevertheless, not only did many professors refuse to comply with the directive, but some of them even wrote protests threatening litigation if the administration should attempt to classify them without their explicit written permission.

The stipulated goal of the Affirmative Action Program, as stated by Dr. Marshak, was "to ensure greater opportunity in employment for minority groups and women." The questionnaire had not included the category "Women," but one may assume that the administration had already assembled or would assemble that information on the basis of social-security data previously in their possession or on the basis of the given names on file. Clearly the intent of the whole program was not "equality" but rather, "*greater* opportunity," with the word *greater,* the adjective serving as the base of the comparison, referring less to the pre-existing situation (i.e., greater opportunity than before) than to the opportunity offered to others (i.e., greater opportunity than that allowed to other groups).

Many observers both inside and outside of the City University system (e.g., the New York Board of Rabbis, which lodged vigorous protests with the new chancellor, Dr. Kibbee) regarded the program (in the manner in which it was actually being implemented) as unconstitutional and undemocratic. It was one thing to rectify inequities wherever they might exist, but quite another to do so at the unjust expense of particular groups, especially at the price of discarding the merit system. One must recall that the whole program rested on an as yet unproven (perhaps implicit) assumption that previous hiring practices *had* reflected bias. A rough survey such as the one being conducted might provide the basis for a start toward an analysis of whether or not prejudice existed within the system, but a simple comparison of the distributional figures with those of the base chosen (i.e., the population of the whole country, that of the state, that of the city, that of the current student body, etc.) could not by itself properly support a charge of bias. Only a comparison of the percentage hired of qualified minority-group people who had actually applied for the jobs with that of the others who had applied could begin to suggest the true picture.

The questionnaire itself had been crudely devised. Certainly the basis (or bases) of the categories chosen had not been made explicit. Nor had directions for classification been included. Why, for example, was the person filling out the paper restricted to *one* category. Surely, for example, there must be black people born in Puerto Rico. Did one have to make an either-or type of choice, defining oneself *either* as black *or* as Puerto Rican, but not as both? If so, why? Also, how would the offspring of, say a Venezuelan and an Italian classify himself, quite apart from his skin color? Assuredly the breakdown as specified was rather less than ideal. Also, what was the basis of selection of the classificational criteria chosen, which apparently included skin color, some rather vague geopolitical groupings, and sex? Why, for instance, were Hispanic groups split into Puerto Rican and "Other Spanish"? Why not Columbian, Venezuelan, and so on, if geography was the consideration? If cultural complex was the basis for the Puerto Rican-vs.-Other-Spanish split, then clearly a far more sophisticated approach seemed imperative. By either criterion Italian-Americans, as well as the other Americans of foreign descent, should also have been split into additional subgroups (i.e., Neapolitan, Sicilian, etc.). One assumes that the administration would justify the particular choices of geographically-based classes (Puerto Rican, Italo-American, Other Spanish) by means of some statistical measure, thus explaining away the lumping together of Irish, German, Greek, and additional groups under the all-inclusive "Other—Specify" category. Furthermore, a major basis of real discrimination of the past in this country and elsewhere had been religion. Why had the classificational scheme omitted religious groupings? The answer that occurred to many observers, of course, had been the likelihood that this particular affirmative-action program had as its goal the protection and advancement of only certain preselected minority groups, not all. Thus it was discriminating against some groups at the expense of others.

Parallel to the preparation and distribution of the faculty questionnaires, a similar set was printed out for students. A prompt, alarmed reaction from various community groups prevented any but the most limited distribution of these forms. What, asked faculty, students, parents, and others, was the intent of this inquiry? Under open admissions *any* high school graduate could enter the City University, hence an attempt to gain distributional equivalence with some segment of the population might have to focus on excluding rather than admitting representatives of appropriate groups—surely an improper suggestion. Likewise, rumors circulated about a planned program of busing to achieve "proper" distribution among the different municipal institutions. Eventually the administration announced that the questionnaires had been devised purely for the purpose of obtaining educational statistics with the intent of monitoring the effectiveness of the open-admissions program. Although this assertion met with some skepticism—particularly in view of the concurrent faculty questionnaires and their stipulated intent—nevertheless, since the distribution of the student questionnaires ceased, so did much of the public reaction.

Eventually the University Faculty Senate repudiated the negative bias implicit in the misguided implementation of the Affirmative Action Program. It was proper to take steps to prevent bias. It was *not* proper to institutionalize the negative bias of preferential treatment. Despite the later public statements of policy of the Senate, however, at least some administrators apparently did not agree with such a position, and much was taking place behind the scenes, far more than was readily apparent. A good deal of planning, in fact, was actually being conducted in secret whether by deliberate intent or by oversight. In any event, briefed privately, and with nothing put into writing, chairmen called meetings of their departments and informed them of the need to bring the faculty representation of minorities (i.e., certain minorities) and women into alignment with stipulated percentages: thirty percent for women, ten percent for blacks, and so forth. One small language department which included Chinese language and literature among its offerings had three native Orientals on its staff. Would it have to fire two (or perhaps two and a half?) of them to bring its Oriental distribution into line with the desired figures? The department also included one black woman who taught Swahili. Should she count toward the thirty percent figure for women or the ten percent for black—or both?

The word-of-mouth directive called for the department to indicate how they would respond to and implement the Affirmative Action Program. Light banter and semihumorous observations masked the genuine concern of at least some faculty members at one meeting. Where would this program end, and how much was going on that the staff didn't know? Only here and there was explicit information leaking out. It may prove enlightening, therefore, to consider at least a few details of just one of the several proposed plans for implementing the program that did become known, namely the one drawn up at Brooklyn College by the Associate Dean of Faculties, Clyde Dillard.

In his rather extraordinary document, entitled "A Five Year Affirmative Action Plan," Dean Dillard specified that the objectives were "twofold: (1) to achieve an ethnic balance in the administrative staff and noninstructional staff which reflects the composition of the student body; (2) To secure equitable treatment of women and minority groups in all employment, promotional and tenure precedures." No one, perhaps, would reject the second goal, although one would think that equitable treatment should be accorded to everyone, not just to women and minority groups. As for ethnic balance, however, one wonders about the desirability of periodically changing the college personnel to match the vagaries of a continuously varying student (or other) body. Would not a drop in some ethnic group require the firing of, possibly, competent personnel? Would not an increase in another ethnic group entail a rush to hire personnel to match? What would one do if the pool of potentially available personnel from this group included no one at all with the requisite skills and training; accept applicants anyway, regardless of lack of competence? Also, even if the people in question had the skills, if they knew that they were the only ones available and that the college had to hire them, wouldn't they then be able to dictate their own (perhaps outrageous) terms in salary, level of appointment, teaching load, and so forth? If so, the college would exist in a permanent and intolerable state of crisis—at best. Clearly job protection and merit would have to be abolished to accomplish such a stipulated objective.

Dean Dillard did, in fact, anticipate "a change in the composition of the student body from its present makeup, to one having a 25 percent enrollment of minority group members within five years," and therefore he conceded "that this implementation must involve some compromise between statutory requirements of the Board of High Education for qualifications of staff as well as considerations of union rules and civil service rules. Efforts will be made to secure a more flexible interpretation of the rules." Flexible, indeed! What he meant was that standards would have to drop.

The dean further added, "The individual departments, both instructional and noninstructional, have been urged to abandon the 'color-blind' approach to recruiting and hiring procedures and to make deliberate adjustments in the ethnic composition of their respective staffs." This last point reinforces the need to drop standards, since it further limits the available pool of acceptable personnel, but, of course, it does more than give up on quality of education. It gives up on democracy itself. It constitutes an enforced bias to replace the alleged—but unproven (and probably nonexistent)—bias it was designed to correct.

Other details of Dean Dillard's plan contain additional examples of negative bias. Fortunately alert members of the faculty and student body heard about the program and brought it to the attention of the members of the community, whence emerged a real public battle, over the objections of the university administration, to prevent this "Affirmation Action" from going into effect. As seen, the program would be harmful:

(a) to the personnel—teachers, administrators, and other members of the staff—since it would abolish the merit system and tenure in favor of an ever-changing game of matching musical chairs;

(b) to the level of scholarship, since teachers of less competence would necessarily have to be hired in at least certain instances;

(c) to the students, since their education would suffer from the lowered standards;

(d) to the general public, since it depends upon the educational institutions to turn out well trained graduates to provide the services and skills it requires; and ultimately

(e) to the basic concept of democracy, since it advocates "preferential treatment"—a thinly disguised cover for bias, albeit reverse bias.

Lest one naively assume that the cases made here need merely be pointed out for them to receive universal acceptance, with a consequent correction of the reverse bias implicit in the proposed programs of implementation, it may be worth noting part of the reply of one (black) dean at Brooklyn College to a statement by that college's Geology Department to the effect that, although it supported efforts "to end this nation's legacy of discrimination with respect to race, religion, or sex," it nevertheless rejected the Board of Higher Education's proposed program, "which negates the expressed objective of equality and equity." The dean said, "it seems to me that unless some *preferential* treatment is given to these minorities, the initial injustices will never be corrected" and "one cannot talk about equality without at the same time developing the methods of correcting the imbalance. Logically, this imbalance will have to be at the expense of those, who for 400 years have enjoyed the luxuries, richness, and advantages of this country."

In the same letter the dean also employed the stratagem, discussed elsewhere in this book, of attacking as racist anyone disagreeing with his point of view: "Further," he said, "the implications which equate the hiring of minority groups with the lacking of professional ability, in my view, is an extension of some of the racist concepts which this society projects."

One last point deserves attention. Once genuine, not merely purported, bias is prevented from playing any role in the hiring and promotional policies of an institution, then within some reasonable time—namely, that necessary for the acquisition of requisite training where relevant—the personnel distribution should reflect the actual merit and skills of the applicants for the jobs. To the extent that all population groups seek these jobs—but only to that extent—one would expect the personnel figures to mirror the figures for the population as a whole. Recent controversial claims by the psychologist Jensen that one minority group (blacks) lack at least one type of intellectual ability (abstract reasoning) have received wide publicity and have subsequently been debated at length, often with Jensen being denounced as racist. It is not the intent here to analyze the basis of his tentative assertions or of the various possible refutations —although strictly from a scientific view, any refutation should properly take the form not of an appeal to emotions, the United States Constitution, or concepts of equality before the law, but rather of an explicit pinpointing of weaknesses of either his evidence or his reasoning, or else of the conducting of tests and experiments whose results point in another direction. Yet, getting back to the Affirmative Action Program, are not those advocates of preferential treatment, such as the dean, asserting in effect that the minority (or minorities) requiring such special advantage are incapable of competing on an equal basis despite equality of opportunity? When he says, as above, "that unless some preferential treatment is given to these minorities, the initial injustices will never be corrected," is he not also saying that these minorities lack the intelligence to compete on an equal basis, all other things being equal? Jensen, if reports concerning his intent and methods are correct, may well have devised poor or inaccurate experiments, with potentially invalid results, but he was, nevertheless, adhering to at least the outward appearance of a scientific methodology, with his conclusions growing out of his experiments, not out of presuppositions as to what he expected or wanted. The Brooklyn College dean, on the contrary, *was* making an unwarranted (although covert) presupposition about the inability of the minorities. This latter position, it would seem, *is* racist, and any member of the minority in question should as a matter of pride and self-esteem reject this preferential treatment lest his own group acquire a stigma of self-evaluated inferiority, along with the economic and social advantages conferred.* Likewise, so-called "liberals," overly quick to accuse others of racism, might examine their own motivations in insisting on preferential treatment rather than simple equality for these minorities.

*If one should argue—as some have, in fact, argued—that the preferential treatment should be accorded, not because of a fear that the minorities cannot compete, but rather because of an assumption that they deserve reparations for the centuries of enslavement, abuse, and suffering, then this premise should be made explicit and argued on its own merits—if any. Then one might ask why such reparations should be paid by groups which bear no responsibility at all for the ill treatment. Indeed, some groups (e.g., the Jews) may well have endured as much mistreatment or more. Should *these* groups likewise demand reparations—that is, preferential treatment—for that reason? Also, why should these reparations be paid indiscriminately to those who may not have suffered as stipulated? To assert that every member of a minority group has suffered just because of *nominal* membership in the minority is an obvious absurdity.

18. The Demand for Relevance

A major focus of discontent on many American campuses nowadays centers around the demand for "relevance." Students praise or damn courses, subjects, and the professors who give or discuss them with the catchwords—perhaps *battlecries* would be more accurate—"relevant" or "irrelevant." Administrators and even faculty too often play the same game, sometimes for reasons of expediency—to show that they are "with it," sometimes for reasons of muddleheaded thinking.

As used by many students, the term "relevant" often signifies no more than "interesting to me—personally" or "emotionally stimulating." Aside from possible questions of imprecise language, few people if any are likely to object to "relevant courses" in such a sense. Clearly everyone desires better and more stimulating courses where such can be achieved. More often than not, however, the frame of reference is one of short- versus long-term relevance. The students want to see the *immediate* application of everything discussed in the classroom, and unless this practical cause and effect relationship appears at once, to them the material is irrelevant. Also, as Professor Howard Adelson has observed in a private conversation, the topics deemed "relevant" today revolve around a narrow range of political or social problems deemed significant to the students (i.e., ecology, the war in Vietnam, racial or ethnic bias, etc). It was in such a frame of reference that one Professor of English distributed to his colleagues a questionnaire asking if their courses were relevant to a long checklist of problems (e.g., how does your course—Shakespeare, Romantic Poetry of the Nineteenth Century, Chaucer, or whatever —have relevance to problems of the urban ghetto?). As illustrated by this last example, there are assuredly different degrees of relevancy.

Professor Alphonse Juilland, a former chairman of the Graduate Linguistic Committee at Stanford University, has observed that ". . . something is wrong with an institution whose graduates' understanding of relevance coincides with that of freshmen." Yet how much worse is an institution if the faculty's understanding of the concept is likewise the same? A number of professors queried on their understanding of the term *relevant* immediately replied with another question: Do you mean my own use of the word or my students' use? Invariably they snorted in disgust at what they saw as the students' view. Nevertheless, faculty at institutions throughout the country (to be sure, not *this* particular group of faculty, who, by and large, were consulted precisely because I felt that they had better-than-average perspective) have abdicated their decision-making prerogative in favor of giving students "power" so that the as-yet poorly educated students might somehow shape the institutions and the courses for greater relevance. Yet by handing over this power, are not the faculty and administrators in effect replacing their own (presumably) better informed perspective with the students' as yet limited and short-range views?

Often one cannot see the connections among apparently disparate facts or views until after one has acquired a broader educational background. Furthermore one's capacity even to respond emotionally or intellectually to many topics rests directly on one's ability to make these connections. Hence many students would rule out as "irrelevant" (in the inexact but widely used evaluative sense) courses and subjects which they might find exciting once they have acquired this foundation—a foundation which is, in my view, one of the major functions of a liberal education (as opposed, say, to a trade-school training). Too many students today suffer from what Professor Robert Hennion of the City College of New York has called the "fallacy of unique experience"—the view that the problems which they face have never been encountered before. The students, locked into their own vacuum of temporal and geographical provinciality, lack the knowledge that other people have encountered and dealt with many of the same problems, and these students suffer, therefore, from an inability to profit from the experience of other people. Professor Hennion has introduced a course into the City College curriculum *specifically* designed to show that people of the ancient world *have* grappled with many of the problems viewed by the students as exclusive to their own time and place (cf. the Roman poet Juvenal on urban problems, or the Greek historian Thucydides on men's motivations or on the ecological balance between resources and population).

Invariably, although the wording differed, most of the great teachers and scholars I consulted on *their* view of relevance had a long-range view. Indeed, in their opinion, the very purpose of higher education is the development of the ability to comprehend principles and make generalizations that may very well have immediate applicability but which go beyond any one short-range problem. Professor Marnin Feinstein of the City College saw the goal of an education as the broadening of one's "understanding of the world" and the acquisition of the ability "to think" and "grasp problems." Relevance might be gauged against the background of *this* measure. When asked to justify (i.e., specify the relevance of) a particular course, Professor Feinstein replied that it provided "links in the chain of civilization" and that an overview of the "continuity of that linkage" constituted part of a genuine education. Professor Harry Levtow of the English Department, when asked for a justification (in terms of relevance) of the teaching of literature, noted, as an example, that through the study of specific works one might come to an understanding of the difference between conscious and subconscious motivations—the fact that a person might know the distinction between good and evil but not always be in control of his own motives. Here again was a reaching out for the generalization that transcends the specific facts. Yet one requires a broad base of hard facts before one has enough data from which to extrapolate.

Other scholars had also noted—independently—the political and social nature of some of the students' concept of relevance as mentioned by Professor Adelson. Professor Juilland, for instance wrote the following:

> The most concrete understanding of relevance is in a political and social context: much academic work appears irrelevant to students, and to some teachers too, in that it does not aim expressly at altering the fabric of the nation. This kind of relevance could be satisfied only by converting colleges and universities into deliberate tools of economic, political, and social reform. However worthy such conversion may appear to some, it violates the tacit "social contract" on the basis of which societies grant institutions of higher learning the kind of freedom we call "academic." To oversimplify its terms, the contract authorizes members of the Academy to follow their endeavors wherever they may lead, provided they do so in pursuit of the truth. It grants both scholars and students an immunity of sorts: society shall not hold them accountable for the practical consequences of academic activities which are not moved by the express intent to change the political and social arrangements of the community.

Obviously, of course, many students and academicians, seeing the campus as a testing ground for social engineering, have violated the implicit terms of this unwritten agreement. Juilland suggests that, if the "tacit contract" is unacceptable, it should be made explicit—"and explicitly cancelled."

Professor James Mirollo, Chairman of the Graduate Department of English and Comparative Literature at Columbia University, noted in a private conversation that this focus on the "relationship to social reality" often "excludes . . . the aesthetic sphere." Although this aesthetic may not have a direct utilitarian value, it does constitute "a human good." When asked to justify the study of Dante from the viewpoint of "relevance," Dr. Mirollo observed, among other measures, what one can learn from that writer's value as "a great moralist."

As understood by this writer and by others, one central focus pursuit of higher education, perhaps its very *raison d'être*, is the free pursuit of long-range understanding. The short-range view that would demand that a course, say in medieval history, should solve the immediate problem of sewage disposal or income taxes is part of a general trend seen all too often nowadays—a childish demand for instant gratification, an impatience which ignores the facts and perspective that only a genuine and broadbased background can bring, one which taps the collective wisdom of the millennia, of the painful, slow development of civilization itself. There is, to be sure, nothing wrong with or demeaning in short-term goals and short-range perspective—after all one does have to fix the plumbing, clear away the garbage, and otherwise deal with the immediate necessities of life. Yet, as the upward climb of civilization has demonstrated over and over again, the nonutilitarian often has eventual (and greater) relevance even in the utilitarian sphere. Benjamin Franklin's classic response to an eighteen-century version of the relevancy question might be kept in mind. When asked, in that oft quoted episode, for the practical use of electricity, he replied, "Madame, what use is a newborn baby?" Yet what utilitarian ends does electricity now serve? Our civilization could hardly function without it. Yet to Franklin its study constituted a purely intellectual pursuit—one that would surely be viewed as irrelevant by those who prefer the short-range measure of value.

19. The Cumulative Chain Reaction

The open-admissions predicament, pointing the way to a future possibility wherein doctoral degrees may be granted for political not educational reasons, justifiably raises the questions of where the process starts and where does it—or can it—end. As seen with the subcommittees to consider the admission of minority groups to the graduate programs, each step appears no greater than its predecessors, but the cumulative result is disastrous. It is easy to see how the mass influx of poorly prepared students can undermine standards, thus the pressures to graduate, if not all of those entering, at any rate large numbers of still uneducated pupils. Once the level of low competence is accepted as a norm, the next pressure, already seen, propels the same forces into and through the graduate schools.

Although occasional popular articles in magazines or newspapers may touch on the decline of the schools and the products of these schools, there has been little in the way of solid documentation of what is happening. What is more, there is not likely to be any such evaluation for the simple reason that, in many subjects, marking is a comparative process. It presupposes a regularity of some hypothetical base-level. Until recent times, statistically, any one given class of students contained roughly the same distribution of abilities as any other class. To be sure, during some given term a particular section might contain a few more individuals brighter than was typical, but such variations in ability would average out over the long span of time. Thus, the teacher would have a continuing sense of what could be expected from the members of the class. He could note any deviations from that base and assess his students realistically. Even if a few underprepared students did appear in his classroom, he would readily spot them by virtue of the continued presence of either average or, occasionally, superior students. When *large* numbers of inadequately trained students appeared all at once, however, he was subject to a subtle misjudgment resting on a dislocated median line.

Only at the very start of the downgrading of standards would the change be evident, since the teacher's orientation would still rest on the norms of the immediately preceding term. Thus, at City College, one history professor noted a pupil's complaint: the latter couldn't understand the lecture because the words were "too hard." Such a student would never have been in that teacher's audience at all before. Despite disclaimers to the contrary, by the new criteria for measurement, a class of nonreaders—many subliterate, some possibly even illiterate—were filling the seats. During the first such term, a conscientious teacher would be appalled, but would still carry on by the old measures of achievement. After awhile, unfortunately, he would find himself unconsciously choosing "simpler" vocabulary, giving shorter reading assignments, and generally pacing his presentation to the more limited capacities of his audience. It can be predicted that within a brief time any student who by previous measures would have just been an average student will be receiving straight As in his courses. The new average C student will be at a competence level that previously would not even have gained him admittance to the class.

The most striking *reductio ad absurdum* of the process will be the consequences in the sciences. Who, for example, would care to undergo a kidney operation by someone who can barely tell the kidney from the liver? If that illustration is too extreme, consider driving an automobile over a bridge designed by someone who was weak in the computation of stress loads. Such a person would never have been licensed before. Tomorrow he will be a straight-A student by virtue of the comparative ignorance of his classmates. Indeed, within the foreseeable future the potential boards of examiners in these or other fields may themselves be so poorly trained that they will not even recognize incompetence when they see it.

Strangely enough, some educators see the consequences of what they themselves are supporting for political reasons, and they say, "Well, we'll have to hold the line in at least those fields where public safety is at stake." Yet their position is invalid here on two counts, not just one.

The first is that the line is *not* being held even in those fields as critical as medicine. For example, Brooklyn College of the City University of New York had had for some years an arrangement with one medical college whereby a definite though gravely limited number of entrance places were reserved for Brooklyn College students, whose selection rested squarely on a highly competitive merit system.* Although there was no special provision for students from minority groups, membership in a minority was no disqualification either. Only the brightest students received the scholarships. Furthermore, this initial selectional process did not in itself guarantee a medical degree. The students had to live up to their promise, or out they went. The drop-out rate was high.

A few years ago, because of pressures for greater ethnic and racial balance, the medical school cut into the very limited number of general Brooklyn College openings to guarantee twelve acceptances to minority-group students—regardless of how these students ranked competitively with the full range of applicants. Perhaps some of the minority students would have made it anyway via the old

*Both arrangements, the earlier and the later, were tacit rather than formal, but the source of this information was quite explicit. The students were "poverty area students from EOP and SEEK," remedial programs in City University. The author has heard reports of similar groups of previously deficient minority-group students being accepted by other medical schools via competition-bypassing routes and then doing better (according to their retention rate—an indirect variety of academic score card) not only than could be expected in light of their own earlier records but better even than their classmates who had entered medical school by the usual competitive channels. One such report elatedly attributed the extraordinary results to "motivation." The author, although greatly desirous of being reassured on the validity of this sudden and unforeseen spurt in competence, reserves judgment: the usual substance of medical schools requires a sound grounding in various prerequisites—scientific disciplines that are not picked up by simple eagerness or wishful thinking. Unfortunately the only way that the real qualifications of the students can be ascertained would be by extensive independent testing, since the marks given by overly sympathetic teachers or else teachers fearful of being called "biased" may not be an accurate reflection of the real situation.

competitive route, but most certainly others would not. They, nevertheless, were now being accepted *in preference to more qualified students*. If the story ended there, one could write it down as a simple negative quota system, but the pernicious momentum went beyond mere discrimination no matter how well intentioned. It continued (and possibly still continues) to protect the minority-group students through their course work. As suggested, even the brighter group could expect some failures in the normal sequence of events. Yet one report indicated that not one single minority-group student had been dropped for failure so far as could be ascertained up to the time of that inquiry (1971). Is it plausible that less qualified students should be better than their more qualified and talented classmates? Obviously not! At least some students who are undoubtedly doing failing work are being pushed through medical school. Does the *reductio ad absurdum* of the kidney operation still seem too extreme?

The second objection to the statement about holding the line in "critical" areas represents the obverse of the coin. Does this position entail the dropping of standards in "noncritical" fields? Who is to define "critical," and, of greater consequence, by what right are other areas being downgraded? Is there no fraud in offering a pseudo- rather than a true education, regardless of what the field or subject matter may be? Has the educational establishment—whatever that mythical creature may be—become so cynical that it can even pay lip service to fraud and deceit?

Those at each level in the complex chain of education regularly point to the next lower rung in the ladder as the hideous cause of failure. Thus the colleges point to the high schools; the latter point to the junior schools; the junior high schools point to the elementary schools, and the first-grade points to the kindergartens, whose teachers say the children come from disadvantaged homes, from slums, overcrowding, malnutrition, and so on. Ultimately all society stands indicted because Johnny can't read. Yet it is also true that years ago the background disadvantages of some of the starting pupils were infinitely greater. Today, although there may not be great luxury, few children actually suffer genuine privation: the welfare authorities assure at least a minimal diet, clothing, and shelter. Indeed many of today's welfare recipients have television sets, hi-fi's, and other conveniences that would have been regarded some decades ago as indescribable luxuries even by the well-to-do. Yet decades ago children who did not even know English somehow started through the school system and, even though they did not always stick with it nearly as long as now seems the norm, these offspring of immigrant parents somehow learned English, mastered their multiplication tables, and went on to become the doctors, lawyers, and businessmen that make up our society. In those days there was genuine hunger, and deprivation, and discrimination too, but when a child received failing marks no militant parent group assailed the teacher. Instead parent and child agonized over the subject, placing the responsibility squarely on the child who was given to know that *he* had to measure up to par, not that he was the victim of society, a wicked school system, teachers who didn't understand him, or any of the other pseudosociological nonsense now handed out.

In one particular sense and only one, the educational system does hold primary responsibility. In all other respects the system can only make the environment more favorable to learning. That primary blame is the failure to inculcate self-responsibility in the student as early in the process as possible. This self-responsibility is *not* the same as the pride which many parents and educators insist on, perhaps rightfully, since the latter sometimes takes the form, "My heritage is great; therefore if I fail, *you* or society must be at fault, not I." The self-responsibility would call for a response, "If *I* failed, you or society may or may not have contributed to that failure, but *I* bear the disgrace and therefore *I*'ll work harder and, one way or other, *I*'ll overcome my own deficiency."

It is true that some children reach the starting point of the school system in a mental state more conducive to good learning than others do. This statement has always been true. It is what happens after the children start school that must be of central concern to educators since the school system cannot act upon the children before then. Ironically enough, part of the chief causes of the aggregative and cumulative failure of the schools arose as a result of an efficiency-directed move—one designed to save waste effort and needless bookkeeping.

At one time a student would never have been promoted from one class to another if he had not passed the work of the lower-level course. If he failed, he was held back until he made up the work he was required to know. This policy made sense and indeed was the only prudent program to follow in a system where so much of the work was sequential. One cannot handle algebra, for example, before one has mastered elementary arithmetic—adding, subtracting, multiplying, and so on; nor can one handle elementary physics or chemistry until one can solve a simple equation. Likewise, one cannot handle assignments in literature or history until one can read with adequate speed and sufficient comprehension. These facts are well known and seemingly should be self-evident. Yet they were ignored because of the impersonal bureaucracy embedded in a ponderous, slow moving, unresponsive organizational setup. In 1956 the Board of Education abolished by decree the semiannual structuring of New York's elementary schools. Thus, instead of dividing the seventh-year classes into 7A and 7B sections, the new structuring grouped the entire seventh-year pool of students into one single level. Presumably at midyear (i.e., the academic year—that is, around January) the class would be midway through the seventh-year work. However no one could be promoted into this seventh term (year-long term) until the end of the academic year so that he could start in September with the others.

By the earlier arrangement, one could have started 7B in either September or in January. By the new arrangement there was no 7B at all; hence one could only start the entire seventh grade (the old 7A *and* 7B combined) in September.

The intent of the new dictum was to cut down on the paper work involved in maintaining the A and B dichotomies and also to simplify the administrative practice with regard to assignment of teachers to A or B sections. On paper the reorganization made excellent sense. The consequences of this seemingly reasonable directive, however, contributed tremendously to the degeneration of the entire eduational sequence.

Now to hold back a student, say for 7A, meant that the student would have to wait not just the two or three months for the next 7A class to start, but for close to a year to elapse before the combined seventh-grade class began again. If, perchance, the failing student were in what once had been a B-section—say 7B—he would have to repeat not merely the work up to that point for the 7B part but also all of what had once been 7A. Obviously a poor student—the one likely to fail—would already be out of place in his own class. To put him back and force him to repeat work he had already had while bearing the stigma of having been left back both alienated *and* bored him. Thus he became not merely a troubled child, in need of aid, but a disruptive child as well, because of his double problem.

To retrieve the situation and minimize the consequences, it was decreed that a student would only be left-back once. Hence, after this edict, if a student had already been held back one year he could never again be subject to pressure to make him do his work.

Within a short time, teacher after teacher was reporting how one student or another was sneering at him or her, saying, in effect, "You can't hold me back since I already was held back before. Therefore, I'll damn well do as I please." The result of the policy was devastating at two levels. The first was the immediate reaction of the substandard pupils who now had no reason—so they thought—to work hard. These students then were locked into a treadmill to academic and eventually to socioeconomic disaster since they then had to mark time until old enough to get out of school, virtual illiterates. At least *prior* to open admissions, however, a few of the more ambitious students could be brought back on the academic path with the potentiality of being admitted to college *if they raised their marks.*

20. Fiscal Responsibility and Irresponsibility

Most, possibly all, institutions of higher learning in this country find themselves in serious financial difficulty. A few have already failed and closed their doors. Others are about to. Even without additional complications—which are many, some of them self-inflicted—the simple existence of an inflationary economy would continuously escalate the regular, fixed costs of education. In the past, these institutions have necessarily had to rely on endowments, contributions from alumni, grants from philanthropic foundations, and on other, outside sources of income to make up the difference between the actual, total expenses and the amounts derived from tuition. Although the costs of tuition may seem enormous to those who have to pay them, few, if any, institutions have ever received, via this source, more than half of their real expenses. Consequently, *any* unnecessary increase in costs starts an educational institution on the path toward financial disaster and ultimate oblivion. Obviously some institutions have more limited resources than others, hence must be more prudent than their more affluent sisters.

The simple replacement expenses incurred at many campuses as a result of riots and deliberate destruction (e.g., bombings, arson, "trashing" of offices, breaking of windows) have been painful, far beyond the direct impact via disruption of the educational process itself. Worse yet, insurance companies have raised their rates in geometric proportion to the damage done. In some instances, as at

City College, where there has been a complete breakdown of law and order, with both thefts and armed robberies becoming commonplace, insurance companies have withdrawn their coverage altogether—at any price. In addition, many institutions have had to employ private protection agencies to police their property. All of these factors, and others which are related (e.g., the need to pay higher salaries to tempt faculty to risk teaching there), have played a role in pushing the schools to the brink of financial disaster. The reluctance to call public law enforcement agencies promptly in response to actual damage or clearcut threats of destruction, then, has denied these institutions part of the financial relief they might have gained. The argument that human beings are more important than "mere" property will neither restore an institution that is forced to close because of economic failure nor will it provide an education for those students who will suffer as the result of such closure. This misguided humanitarianism directed toward self-avowed revolutionists and self-centered militants represents not higher "human values" but a total lack of responsibility toward the *non*revolutionists and the *non*militants: it is a course of action geared to depriving *them* of *their* rights.

Beyond this, many radical or liberal faculty members and administrators have displayed additional irresponsible attitudes that defy belief. The range and nature of their actions vary widely. Those employed by public institutions have treated the funds provided by taxing other people as inexhaustible sources of income which can—so they think—never be depleted. For example, at the City University of New York, the expenses incurred in making the Graduate Center at Forty-second Street a plush model of stylistic elegance and comfort would make any cost accountant blush. A member of the Board of Higher Education who absolutely insisted on more rather than less expensive furnishings at the center, however, is the same person who refused to allow a contract to be assigned for the rapid construction of the classrooms that were so desperately needed at Brooklyn College to accommodate the additional students to be admitted under open enrollments. This member, incidentally, also sat on the board which mandated this open-admissions policy, without reference to or consideration of the imminent bankruptcy of New

York City, which would have to foot the bills. The chancellor of that university, who also had pushed for open admissions, despite the potential costs, was granted a blanket sum of more than half a million dollars in addition to other funds to help develop the new program. He allocated this amount to the building of elegant *homes* for the presidents of the City University colleges and for himself. It cost the city $180,000 for his own house alone. Yet only a few months later he was to direct public charges of immorality toward those in the city and state fiscal agencies who refused to allocate all of the additional funds which he wanted for running the university. The fact that these funds were completely unavailable without any further taxation of an already overtaxed citizenry seemed beyond his comprehension. Thus, Chancellor Bowker and the Board of Higher Education actually threatened to close down the university completely rather than run it on a more modest budget. One may speculate on how many students might have been educated for the $180,000 spent on the chancellor's new home. Yet it would perhaps be unfair to suggest selfishness as the chancellor's motive. Undoubtedly Dr. Bowker was looking to the future and to the dignity of the chancellor's office even after he should leave that spot. In point of fact, he *did* announce his intention to resign, an intention which somehow coincided chronologically with the first public disclosures of his fiscal irresponsibility. He announced that he was moving on to California where greater educational challenges awaited him. A liberal press lamented his departure. It did not, however, reveal why California offered a greater challenge than New York. Bowker, it said, had ushered in the glorious promise of open admissions. No one asked who was going to make open admissions work or extricate the New York system from the morass into which Bowker's irresponsible actions had plunged it. New York had open admissions—and the imminent likelihood of no school system at all. Regardless of aspirations, there is an order of priorties that must be considered only after realistic examination of the fiscal resources available for a purpose.

A different type of irresponsibility may be seen in the action of certain radical faculty members and administrators at Clark University in Worcester, Massachusetts. Recognizing the problems of the black minority of the country, this group set out to recruit black students for Clark. Prior to this time, the number of such students had been rather small for the simple and self-evident reason that the black population of Worcester numbered less than one percent of the total. Thus to induce black students to come to Clark, a team of recruiters had to search beyond the Clark area, offer scholarships covering tuition, room and board, and traveling expenses, and the institution somehow had to get the money for these scholarships. The recruitment and the assignment of funds *preceded* the acquisition of those funds. Thus an attempt was made to tax the faculty a certain percentage of their salaries to provide the money needed. Some faculty members refused to pick up this gratuitous charge. Many were willing to contribute to a general fund for *all* needy students without regard to race, but not to a fund for blacks alone—a type of scholarship which they saw as a negative quota system. They had no objections to the distribution of all of the available funds to blacks if it should turn out that black students were the only ones in need of assistance, but they were unwilling to institutionalize a variety of racism. Thus this source of fund raising—the taxing of faculty members—failed to balance the Clark budget. Yet, even if the contributions had been made, the sum total would still have been inadequate to the multiplying costs, because of the commitment they had made to continue the old scholarships through sophomore, junior, and senior years (or more if need be) while regularly admitting additional scholarship students. The crowning irony came when a critical mass of such entrants had been admitted. The radical faculty members had expressly sought out militant blacks, not "Uncle Toms." The militants, with the aid of some outsiders not enrolled in the university, forcibly seized the administration building. Among their demands (nonnegotiable, of course) was one for *additional* scholarships for militant black students. The administrators agreed, although, at the moment, they already had pledged more money than they had any likelihood of raising. Their generous good will may put the institution out of business altogether within the foreseeable future.

21. Faculty Who Advocate Lawlessness: A Critical Turning Point

There is a peculiar quirk to the minds of academicians which makes these otherwise rational scholars particularly vulnerable to certain catch phrases and high-sounding slogans. Just as Pavlov's dogs were once conditioned by the great psychologist to salivate to the stimulus of a bell even though the food that previously had accompanied the ringing no longer was forthcoming, so have many academicians been conditioned to react to words such as "freedom of speech." Such college professors respond emotionally to phrases, and, thus, cease to use their powers of reason, even though, in actual fact, the stimulus may really be wielded by those who desire to destroy, not preserve, the precious "freedom" the scholars rightfully hold so dear.

It is a widely recognized phenomenon that not only would the violent disruptions on many campuses not have gotten as far as they have without the tacit consent or even connivance of some faculty members, but in at least certain instances trouble has been instigated and fed by the words and acts of revolution-minded members of the teaching staff. These advocates of lawlessness see the university as a forum for the righting of the problems of the world. There is, of course, room for dissenting judgments regarding the primary and secondary functions of the universities. Yet all too many of those desiring to change the world via the campus do not cavil at the use of illegal, often deadly and destructive, tactics. They actively promote willful vandalism, hooliganism, intimidation, and even assault and murder. What is ironic, however, is their thus far well-founded confidence that, having urged others on to commit felonious acts often aimed at the curtailment of the rights of their victims, they can legally hide behind the American right of freedom of speech. They claim that *they*—personally—stayed within the law: they *merely* talked others into the performance of criminal activities. They assert that the Bill of Rights guarantees *them* the freedom to say what they want, even if the consequences of their speeches are illegal.

What is appalling is not so much that the law is not always too clear on this point—i.e., Oliver Wendell Holmes once asserted that "freedom of speech" does not include the right to cry "Fire!" in a crowded theater, yet the formal, legal establishment of the tenuous line between dangerous license in the use of speech and simple "freedom" is difficult to pin down in a court of law (the Supreme Court decision in *Brandenberg* vs. *Ohio,* 395 US 444, is relevant here)*—but rather the inappropriate ways in which honest, nonrevolutionary faculty have reacted to the performance of their more unscrupulous colleagues. However, even if the legal picture is contradictory, confusing, and uncertain thus far as a guide to restraining criminal *intent,* there is no such difficulty in making crucial distinctions pertaining to the desirability of hiring or retaining as members of the *responsible* academic community those faculty whose orientation is clearly geared to depriving others of the very rights they claim for themselves. Surely the universities, if they are to continue to pose as the bastions of reason, owe it to themselves, not to mention to their constituency—the students—or to the public to reject and cast out from their midst those who reject reason and temperate consideration rather than force and crude disruption as the basis for action.

Unfortunately most efforts to restrain or reject scholars of an illegal turn of mind have inevitably precipitated cries of "repression

*The decision tied together the incitement to commit a crime with the practical test of whether or not any crime actually took place following the incitement.

of free speech!" or "witch hunts!" Often, then, universities have retained the very people seeking to destroy either the university or even society itself, except when, in some instances, determined administrators have resorted to devious tactics to rid themselves of undesirables, employing such subterfuges as "academic judgment" or "scholarship" as the pretexts. Usually such indirect and not strictly honest methods for getting rid of various faculty members have angered the majority of the academic community, who recognize—rightly—the moral weakness of the position. Hence the observers then react with strong emotions to claims that the individuals are being "purged" because of their political beliefs. They feel that the fundamentals of freedom are under attack by a fascistic administration and, therefore, misguidedly rally to the defense of democratic principles, never grasping the central fact that the individuals whose rights they so heatedly defend are the very people who would deprive *them* of *their* liberties. Although it is important to remove such people from the academic community, *it is a mistake to do so by subterfuge*. The issue is important enough to face directly, not peripherally. Clearly, of course, those administrators who have acted with the legally available but not always relevant means such as "academic judgment" or "scholarship" have felt—probably accurately—that the rest of academia would desert them if they employed a direct frontal attack on revolutionists on the appropriate grounds of their revolutionary activities—specifically, their incitement to what the present laws define as illegal acts. In such an academic climate the administrators are in a double-bind—damned if they do and damned if they don't. Under these circumstances it is of crucial importance that perspective be brought to the problem so that the conditioned reflexes of academia be geared to the defense of liberty, not to its destruction. Therefore, the case of H. Bruce Franklin marks a possible turning point in this struggle.

On January 5, 1972, a specially convened Faculty Advisory Board at Stanford University finally reached a decision after months of hearings (September 28 to November 5 with final briefs on December 17, 1971) on the matter of the alleged illegal activities of a tenured faculty member and of the action to be taken in respect to these performances. Specifically, the charges against Professor H. Bruce Franklin were four in number:

(1) that on January 11, 1971, he had himself helped to disrupt and that he had induced others to disrupt a scheduled speech by Ambassador Henry Cabot Lodge, thus forcing a cancellation of the meeting and, in effect, *denying to others the right to hear and be heard;*

(2) that at a war-protest rally held on February 10, 1971, he had urged and induced protestors (both students and nonstudents) to disrupt normal university functions by occupying and shutting down the Computation Center;

(3) that he had interfered with police activities aimed at dispersing those who had followed his instigations and unlawfully occupied the center;

(4) that he later, at a rally in the Old Union Courtyard, had "urged and incited students and others to engage in disruptive conduct which threatened injury to individuals and property" (from which activity genuine acts of violence followed).

Reports of the deliberations of the board—including a 50,000 word report obtainable from Stanford University's Office of Public Relations—suggest that the seven members were continuously mindful of the possible reactions of the academic community and that they did more than bend over backwards to ensure that there should be no possible suspicion about the fairness of their proceedings. They asserted their intent "to balance Professor Franklin's rights as an individual against those of others in the university upon whom his conduct may infringe, and against the functional integrity of the Institution." However, "*where there is doubt, such . . . considerations should be applied asymmetrically in Professor Franklin's favor.*"

With Professors Donald Kennedy (the chairman) and R. M. Brown dissenting on all but the second charge—that pertaining to the shutting down of the Computation Center—the board upheld the last three charges. They did not sustain the first, the one regarding the disruption of Ambassador Lodge's speech, although they did recognize (1) that the meeting had been disrupted so badly as to require a cancellation before the talk could be given and (2) that Professor Franklin himself had engaged in "loud shouting" at least twice and probably more times when the rest of the audience had been quiet.

The details of the actual activities of Franklin and of the trial are of interest—his attempts to incite hostility against both our government and against the police, his urging of the audiences to commit violent and illegal acts, including some which threatened bodily harm to individuals and damage to property, and so on. His presupposition of imperialistic aims of our country and his invidious and outrageous comparison of the local police force trying to protect people and possessions against the destruction of law breakers with an occupation army deserve clearcut delineation and rebuttal, if only to show the extremist positions accepted as fashionable on some campuses. Yet, what the Stanford board strove most to make clear in its decision was precisely the fact that Professor Franklin's political views had never been on trial. They recognized diversity of views as an asset to a university. It was Franklin's behavior, namely, the "incitement to use of unlawful coercion and violence and increasing the danger of injury to others" which they judged unacceptable. The only speech repressed is that conducive to such ends. As the board pointed out, "such behavior should be restrained; insistence on such standards of faculty conduct will not kill open and robust dissent on this or any other campus. . . . Tolerance of such attacks on the freedom of others, under guise of protecting Professor Franklin's freedom to act as he wishes, would be subversion, not support of true academic freedom and individual rights. It is precisely because unlawful coercion and violence infringe upon the rights of others in the university that the charges against Franklin are such serious ones."

In accordance with their findings then, the board recommended Professor Franklin's dismissal, although two of the members would have preferred a less severe penalty. As the *New York Times* pointed out, however, in an editorial on January 11, 1972, "Their counsel of leniency might be supported had the offense been an aberration of momentary passion. But Professor Franklin's consistent contempt for the foundations of a free, rational and nonviolent community was unmistakably reaffirmed when he responded to the faculty verdict with a call for 'revolutionary counterviolence,' while his wife 'symbolically' stood by his side with a rifle."

Not too surprisingly—at least not surprising to those who know the typical academic mind, subsequent issues of the *New York Times* and of other papers carried angry, highly emotional letters denouncing the verdict. Faculty members throughout the country were aroused to defend—so they thought—freedom of speech, which they felt was being imperiled by the landmark decision. Even one Nobel laureate lent the weight of his prestige to the rejection of this repudiation of a notorious abuse and misuse of freedom. Fortunately, there were others, including another Nobel Prize winner (Dr. Joshua Lederberg), who apparently knew the facts and saw them in perspective.

Although the board's decision is a matter of record, the final and truest judgment—namely, how the rest of the academic world responds to the precedent—still remains to be delivered. If academia fails to employ its collective reason in its own self-defense, one may wonder at its vaunted rationality. Assuredly activities such as Franklin's are antidemocratic, geared to depriving others of *their* rights. Defense of such freedom is misguided and irrational. It can only reflect, as indicated earlier, the conditioned-response syndrome which bypasses reason. Yet would-be agitators and subversives *know* they can rely on an unthinking reflex to key stimuli such as "freedom of speech" or "repression" even when it is they and not their opponents who would repress and even destroy the liberty to which they so glibly refer.*

*Although the hard-core revolutionaries constitute a minority among the faculty, both their colleagues and the general public generally underestimate both their deadly intent and the effectiveness of their commitment. For example, shortly before the violence at Cornell, one instructor, Cleveland Donald (reportedly one of the more extreme black militants), taught one section of a political science class. He spent most of the term discussing white racism. One day, after being particularly stirred up with emotion, a white girl asked, "What can we do to help?"

"Get a gun and start shooting!" came the reply.

This same Cleveland Donald, according to news reports, later addressed a meeting of SDS on the need to step up the violence. The record of the destruction later attributable to SDS requires no comment, not to mention the earlier photograph of black militants at Cornell emerging from a dormitory rifles in hand, a picture which captured headlines all over the world.

22. Amnesty: Invitation to Disaster

One—often nonnegotiable—demand tacked on to the others in innumerable confrontations is the call for amnesty—an insistence that those who seize or burn buildings, destroy property, or harm faculty and students not be held accountable for their actions, that they not be penalized in any way for their lawless deeds. Yet this demand encountered more and more frequently on campus—particularly as the agitators who travel from campus to campus become known—hardly differs from the general tendency seen in society as a whole. It constitutes part of what may be properly called "a cult of irresponsibility." It fits together with other characteristics of a permissive society such as the leniency of the courts which blame the "wicked" society for a criminal's felonious acts (e.g., murder, rape, or mugging) rather than the wrongdoer himself, with a consequent freeing or, at the least, reduction of the sentence of the culprit, or, alternatively, a freeing of offenders proven guilty beyond any shadow of doubt because of some technicality such as an alleged failure to warn them of their rights before interrogation. The rioters at Attica, sparked by avowed revolutionists, also demanded amnesty. The draft evaders who fled the country to avoid the service accepted by other young Americans likewise have their defenders who advocate amnesty. This book, of course, by its very nature precludes any extensive digression such as would be necessary to deal with these and other reflexes of the same pattern beyond the brief observation that the demand for and expectation of amnesty on the nation's campuses represents the same fundamental moral decay that has spread through much of society, not just the more narrow segment discussed here.

A good part of the destructive frenzy that has taken place in our colleges and universities would have fizzled and died had both administrators and faculty presented a united front in condemning the activity rather than offering vacillation or equivocal statements about the "high motivations" of the rioters, most of whose leaders have an arrogant assumption of their own intellectual superiority—hence a presumed right to do as they please and a near psychotic reaction to restraints of any manner, shape, or form. It is clear, likewise, that even when some faculty and administrators took a firm stand their position was largely undercut by the presence of others—again both faculty and administrators—whose response gave student anarchists a justification for assuming that if *some* of the latter group supported their position it must hold merit, even if disputed.

Academicians must not confuse—as they have confused—their support for any of the pretexts for violence with a support for the violence itself. Furthermore they must make this distinction eminently clear to would-be anarchists. The granting of amnesty, except in the most extraordinary circumstances, obliterates the distinction. It says, in effect, that because a group deplores, say, racism in South Africa or a war in Asia that they have a moral justification to throw a professor down a flight of stairs or burn a building or destroy some scholar's lifetime's work. Under no circumstances do they have a justification for committing an illegal or immoral act, regardless of their claims of provocation.

Those who have personally viewed some of the violence on campus—the obscene mouthings, the emotional outbursts, the breaking of windows, the throwing of rocks at police and others, and all of the other activities never quite comprehended until actually experienced—usually have come away aghast at what they have seen. The parents of the "students," of course, say "My little Janice wouldn't do *that*" or "My Harvey must have been terribly provoked; he is such a quiet boy." Yet these mothers and fathers would never recognize their Janices or Harveys when the latter became part of an irrational mob. To be sure, learned treatises have dealt with mob psychology, but the nature of the situation is not one that words can readily convey. To equate such activity with political protest shows an unbelievable lack of understanding.

There are on many (most?) campuses academicians—or pseudoacademicians—who revel in the violence and excitement. They like to play at revolution. Many of them undoubtedly are radicals who never had the nerve to commit the same acts when they were youths, and so now they enjoy the ferment vicariously, supporting, directly or indirectly, or even instigating the law breakers. These so-called academicians, of course, firmly support calls for amnesty. Another section of this book deals with faculty who want violence, but here suffice it to say that their colleagues must override such support (and eventually get rid of such faculty as well).

Some arguments for amnesty for students represent a position that virtually allows unbridled license to anyone enrolled at college. Yet by what reasonable premise does mere payment of a bursar's fee exempt anyone from the normal rules of human conduct? By such reasoning anyone contemplating rape, murder, or robbery need only enroll at his local college to be allowed to go about his felonious activity unmolested. If caught in the act, he can then say, "But I'm a student" and be excused thereby. The no-police-on-campus syndrome is part of the same irrational position.

A good part of education is concerned with cause-and-effect relationships. For example, if one puts two chemicals together in a specifiable ratio, a predictable reaction takes place. It has, of course, been noted by some observers that a greater number of the anarchists are students majoring in liberal arts rather than those majoring in engineering or scientific fields. Possibly one may attribute the disparity to the fact that the scientists and engineers have fewer illusions about cause and effect, and, therefore *expect* to be held responsible for their own actions. Regardless of the explanation, the offering of amnesty amounts to a removal of the normal effect from the cause. At least until recently, in civilized societies criminal activities have resulted in corresponding punishments, usually geared to the nature of the crime. Furthermore, despite misguided claims to the contrary, the laws governing crime and punishment defined the limits of acceptable and unacceptable behavior and served as a deterrent to criminal activity.

The goals of any decent education surely include the sense of self-discipline and self-responsibility. The offering of amnesty for irresponsible acts not only negates any such goals, but actually serves to produce the reverse. In addition, amnesty is a clear invitation to future lawlessness.

In one of his most famous passages, Shakespeare has Portia argue that "the quality of mercy is not strain'd; it droppeth as the gentle rain from heaven upon the places beneath. It is twice-blest—it blesseth him that gives, and him that takes." With all due respect to the bard as well as to others down through the ages who have argued for mercy, the receiving of amnesty is not a right—and most certainly it should not be granted either alone or as part of a package deal out of fear. Each crime has to be judged on its own merits. Obviously a thoughtless prank should not bear the same penalty as the blowing up of an auditorium or as any other act committed with premeditated destructive intent. The differences can normally be left to the discretion of reasonable judges. However, colleges and universities should have clearcut guidelines to conduct on their premises and such regulations should plainly preclude amnesty. Any policy of amnesty is an invitation to additional felony—an indication that violence, not reason prevails on campus. Surely academia should be the bastion of reason since if reason does not prevail there, where can it survive?

23. The Problem: An Overview

The current, desperate state of American higher education arises from a great number of different, sometimes unrelated underlying causes. Many of these, it is clear, are simply natural phenomena which stem from the explosive growth of population, the administrative problems of providing for and handling the consequent large numbers of students and teachers, the increasing social and sometimes vocational pressures that have driven many youngsters to seek status-conferring degrees despite their own lack of desire for or even their outright antipathy to additional education, the use of the college campus as a legal stratagem for avoiding the draft—hence the presence of still more unwilling, "captive" students in the classrooms—and so on. The perfectly legitimate escalation of the level of aspiration of some minority groups and the associated move toward open-admission policies at various public-supported institutions constitute part of this phase of the problem, at least to the extent that the would-be college- or university-bound applicants have not mastered the knowledge and skills heretofore delegated to the elementary and high-school levels of education. *None* of these "natural" problems are insurmountable; some, in my view, are not even particularly difficult to handle, given proper planning and a reasonable allotment of resources in money, personnel, and space. Later sections of this book will suggest some solutions or at least the types of directions which such solutions may take. In all likelihood, if the educational system survives at all, it will have to be vastly different from that of today. Already mass experiments utilizing newly available technology as well as new combinations of older, well-known techniques are underway in different places both here and abroad. More will be said about this point later.

Thus far I have confined this book to those phases of the problem I have directly observed, or for which information has been readily accessible to me. Nevertheless there is another phase, many of whose consequences have appeared in the foregoing pages, but whose explicit cause has not been expressly stipulated. I must confess to some trepidation at overtly stating that for which proof cannot be demonstrated as readily as for the other assertions made in this volume. Here one arrives at a nebulous area in which speculation and inference must replace concrete evidence. Nevertheless there *is* a chain of solid facts that point in a specific direction, namely that there has been a *deliberate,* centralized plot, emanating from a common source, to overthrow the United States government from within. Statements to this effect have been made by high law enforcement officials of the government and proof of the surmise appears daily in the newspapers—the bombings, the weapons caches discovered, the rhetoric at meetings of militant groups such as SDS, and so on. Books actually written by avowed revolutionists or, alternatively, by militant radicals who have associated daily with such revolutionists have traced the details of plotting and planning, the ebb and flow, the doings of the factions involved. It is the surmise of this observer that the plot has been deliberately planned, instigated, and perhaps, in part, even financed by one or more totalitarian powers which would profit from the downfall of this country. The grand strategy of such a plan encompasses a good deal more than just the educational system, but, since this system is so central to the mental health, moral fiber, and even pragmatic capabilities of the nation, its destruction in whole or part is an important consideration. No claim is made here that enemy agents are necessarily the active executors of the insurrections. Nevertheless, one would have to be willfully blind to avoid recognizing that disgruntled factions of native-born Americans have made regular trips to Cuba, Hanoi, and other Communist-controlled centers and then have returned, stating overtly and in no uncertain terms their intent to further in this country a violent, murderous revolution; of greater consequence, they have followed these statements of intent by real action. Some have, as attested elsewhere, been involved in making and distributing Molotov cocktails, incendiary bombs, and other weapons of destruction. Others have circulated seditious anti-American propaganda assailing our "capitalistic, racist oppressive government." A more select group has visited college campuses throughout the nation in the role of agent provocateurs. Indeed radical contingents on campus have invited people such as Jerry Rubin, Abbie Hoffman, and others of like mind and intent to speak to college groups (usually at outrageous fees). More often than not violence sweeps such campuses directly in the wake of the inflammatory speeches. It is a known fact, but one which is somehow forgotten because of the subsequent events, that Jerry Rubin spoke at Kent State shortly before the first outbursts of violence—the arson, destruction, and so on, which eventually required the presence of the National Guard and led to the tragic consequences which followed. James Michener has indicated in a long two-part article (later made into a book), which he himself researched, how outside agitators converged on Kent and helped stir up the violence. Similar facts can be cited for most of the schools which have suffered disruption, although the scope and extent of such violence has varied from institution to institution.

Not all of those who have participated in one way or another in the events are either Communists or even Communist sympathizers. The effectiveness of revolutionary planning arises from its deliberate use of indigenous scources of dissatisfaction. At one confrontation at City College, the militants split into two factions. One wanted to discuss nothing at all but which buildings would be blown up or burned. A member of this group left the meeting after spouting, in a near psychotic fashion, the most obscene mouthings about the "c——s——ing, f——ing capitalistic imperialistic system," which he was going to help destroy. His statements, apart from the native obscenity, reflected standard Communist dogma. Another rather imprudent militant asserted openly that the School for Black Studies, which constituted one of the "nonnegotiable" demands, would really serve as a school for revolutionists. Other members of the group, who were genuinely interested in such a school as a source of training in the black heritage, were also hostile but were ready to negotiate since *their* real aim was the substance of the demands. When I queried the need for a separate school—which would be autonomous, and thereby not subject to normal academic scrutiny and control—rather than a separate department, which would accomplish the valid goal of providing training in their heritage, the hard-core Communists disrupted the meeting, completely refusing to allow *this* topic to be discussed. Eventually they asserted their intent to murder me. They did not, of course, make clear the fact that they did not want to publicize the difference between their goal—the destruction of America—and that of the black community which was being used.

It is highly doubtful whether any institution has ever existed or even can exist which possesses the power to satisfy everyone in every way. Quite apart from real weaknesses—as here—or injustices, there inevitably are those who feel that they are not adequately appreciated or who are ambitious and covet other positions. These and other groups can be tapped as potential sources of dissatisfaction. Furthermore, *no* course of action can ever preclude disruption when the real intent is the disruption itself rather than the pretext: as already indicated in this book, one Columbia University group of dissidents committed violence because, they claimed, they *didn't* have a recreation room. Another group attacked the same university because the latter was trying to provide a place (the gymnasium) for recreation. It makes no difference what the pretext is—and there is no possible end to pretexts. If one is intent on disruption, one can complain of everything from an invasion of Cambodia to lack of baby sitters for the children of mothers who want to go to school. The variety and scope of the complaints which *have* served on one or another campus as a pretext for disruption surpasses belief. Many rather naive observers assume that most of these confrontations are indigenous and spontaneous. Yet careful reconsideration shows a large undercurrent of planning behind these demonstrations. It would, of course, be impossible to cite outside agitation in *every* single instance. It is doubtful that anyone would make such a claim: there certainly must be local dissatisfactions which erupt from time to time without deliberate outside or inside agitation of any kind. Yet often, even if actual agitation does take place, it cannot always be identified or spotted by investigators. Nevertheless, much evidence does support the likelihood of a well-organized plan of destruction. Once events are set in motion along a certain path there exist enough groups of radical persuasion to carry on with the destruction even when the original agitators withdraw from the action.

Closely associated with such deliberate disruptions, whose aims are destructive rather than constructive, another major cause of the real trouble in the system is the inability or unwillingness of the faculty and administrators to deal with the disruptions. Some of the "nonnegotiable demands," of course, are so patently contrived that only those who are deliberately blind to the truth could possibly ignore the real intent—disruption—rather than the stated pretext. Other demands, as seen, appear quite reasonable, although the instigation of militancy to accomplish the goals likewise may stem from intent to disrupt. As has been shown, often the faculty and adminstrators *do* recognize the pretext for what it is, but they lack the intestinal fortitude to stand up to the disrupters. Sometimes, as at Cornell, they cravenly back down and capitulate to the threat of force although publicly acknowledging the invalidity of the demands. Other times they approve the demands publicly but disapprove privately. On still other occasions, they themselves invent pretexts to justify their approval, often *deliberately* disregarding the available evidence that would necessarily elicit either disapproval or, at the least, public acknowledgement of their own cowardice. Sometimes, they justify their actions, whether to others or to themselves, as matters of practical expediency: they pose as cynical men of a world in which everything is corrupt and in which old-time standards of morality and high principles are merely quaint and old-fashioned. They know in their hearts that they are really seeking plausible justification for their weakness, but they put on a mask to hide from the world—and themselves—the true motivations that dictate their actions.

When the stated goals are seemingly reasonable—although actually only the pretext for trouble—well-meaning, decent students, faculty, and administrators, as well as outside observers (including the media) often genuinely believe in the validity of the pretended goals, and thus allow themselves to be used, not for the rectification of some inequity or injustice or the acquisition of some desirable right, as they think, but rather for the ultimate destruction of America.

If one is to be effective then in saving the American system of higher education, one must keep in mind the very important distinction between the natural problems and those which have been contrived for vicious purposes. One can usually correct the natural problems and also remove the pretexts for some of the complaints; however, one can *never* remove *all* pretexts for destruction or complaint.

Part Two

SOLUTIONS AND NEW DIRECTIONS

24. Recognizing the Dichotomous Nature of the Problem: Prelude to Correction

Education of the future will necessarily differ in very fundamental ways from that of today. It must, if it is to survive at all, become less expensive per segment learned, less time consuming (also per segment but not *in toto*), and, hopefully, more interesting. If extrapolation from present trends may serve as a reliable guide, it will also—quite properly—become a lifelong process, with no artificial upper limit. Later chapters will deal with the reasons, means, and justifications for the types of restructuring that must inevitably come about—the innovations and directions that may already be appearing here and there on the horizon as well as others which will be suggested. The proper start for the reform of the system, however, lies in a direct recognition by administrators of the basic dichotomy already suggested at the end of the last section, namely that between:

(1) the *natural* problems arising from myriad causes, but mainly from (a) an ever increasing population and (b) the raised expectations and aspirations of that population; and

(2) the deliberately fostered problems arising from calculated plans to disrupt or destroy.

Unless administrators recognize this difference between the two kinds of problems and, therefore, act appropriately, American higher education is not only doomed: it may even serve as part of a master plan to help destroy all the rest of the country—a training ground and base for revolutionists whose intent is the demolition of the present form of American government.

The natural problems are formidable enough, but they at least may be treated as challenges to do better and accomplish more. One way or another, they may provide the incentive to higher achievement. The other type of problem, however, poses a threat rather than a challenge under the present conditions—specifically under those conditions in which both administrators and faculty, acting out of cowardice or blindness, either pretend that the second type is really the same as the first, and, consequently, that special *ad hoc* treatment based on good will can eliminate all difficulties or else approach the problem with either a bandwagon mentality (jump on: if you can't lick 'em, join 'em) or an ostrich, head-in-the-ground orientation (if we don't look, perhaps we can pretend that the problem doesn't exist; or better yet, it may go away by itself). There are individuals—unfortunately far too many of them—who have been traitors both to American education and to America itself by virtue of the lip-service which they have paid to revolution. They have pretended that the negative, destructive revolutionary goals were their goals; its aspirations, their aspirations. They have abdicated their own spheres of responsibility and have handed over power to irresponsible or incompetent students or, worse yet, to students or educators intent on something other than the normal goals of education. These moral dropouts have, of course, been too sophisticated to say simply, "We abdicate. We are afraid." Instead they have mouthed phrases such as "progressive innovation" or "relevant restructuring," and, thus, pretended to be doing the same job as before. As indicated in the foregoing sections, other educators—often so-called liberals—reacted inappropriately when their colleagues, who had a greater sense of responsibility than they, sought to call the police or to defend property, lives, or standards. Instead of supporting those who were doing *their* job and thus putting themselves in line for reprisals, some faculty and administrators either reacted to empty cliches such as "no police on campus" or else denounced as reactionary those rare and courageous attempts at maintaining excellence.

If the administration of the future fails, then, to deal appropriately either with the primary threats of deliberate disruption (e.g., the trashing of property, the burning of buildings, the intimidation of personnel) or with the derivative threats (the innumerable faculty and administrative acts that spring from fear), there will be no system worth having or saving. If the administration does handle *these* crises satisfactorily, the in-built ingenuity of faculty and administration can readily handle the more natural problems, some of which will be discussed in the ensuing pages. The situation is and will remain hopeless *only* if educational administrators fail to recognize and face up to the fundamental difference between the two kinds of problem, the natural and the deliberately induced.

25. Reaching Illiterates

As indicated, Johnny can't read. This is a simple, unpleasant, and (to some people) unpalatable fact. The reasons vary. A few have already received consideration, but, regardless of the excuses, the educational problem is not, and should not be, one of simply assigning the blame, but rather of somehow helping Johnny get the training he needs. A second and, from one point of view, far more appalling truth is that there *can't* be enough competent teachers to meet even the regular requirements of the school system, much less the more tantalizing problems of marginal pupils like Johnny. Furthermore, no crash program, regardless of how well devised, can train enough adequate teachers since, as known for some time by psychometricians (those concerned with the scientific measurement of innate aptitudes), the actual distribution of teaching aptitudes in the population as a whole is enormously insufficient for the needs of the country, particularly now that a larger percentage of its members goes to school.* Although some misguided educators talk around or

*In actual fact, the combination of the aptitudes required for success in teaching occurs in such limited distribution that the number of potentially well qualified teachers was necessarily inadequate even *before* the explosive growth of the student population. The psychometric studies, of course, merely confirm what has always been known in an intuitive, perhaps less scientific way—namely that not all of those actually teaching are qualified by nature to act as educators, although, of course, such people can acquire training and technical competence in the subjects they teach. Unfortunately, poor teaching can destroy potentially good pupils as students. It can take all of the joy out of learning.

deny these two facts and thereby obfuscate the central problem, they are merely postponing the inevitable, the need to come to grips with the hard-core, unyielding actuality of the two invariables:

(1) inadequately prepared students (regardless of the reasons for their inadequacy, whether reflecting deficits of training and background or lack of mental capacity), and

(2) inadequate teachers.

Once these twin facts are faced squarely, it becomes possible—although not necessarily easy—to devise the appropriate measures to correct the situation.

If Johnny can't read, it is clear that one urgent priority is to improve his reading skill. Under the present educational setup little real learning can take place until Johnny can read, and, moreover, not merely read haltingly and with difficulty (hence distaste) but read rapidly, with skill and comprehension (hence pleasure and satisfaction). The ability to read well is the single most important skill necessary to academic as well as other success. With this ability someone who is deficient in almost any other subject can pick up the relevant books and catch up rapidly. Without this central tool, most subjects become forever closed to the would-be learner. The urgency of learning to read well varies with the level of the pupil, that is, whether he is in elementary school, high school, or college. Years ago he would never have reached college if he couldn't read. Now the automatic promotion policy adopted in so many public schools and the open college-admissions policy of more recent vintage have brought the nonreader to the doorsteps of the college. Somehow the college must rectify the problem that should have been handled in elementary school. What is more, calling the overworked, harassed, and frustrated elementary-school and high-school teachers names cannot help to educate the new college student. The educators must deal with the situation that actually exists, not waste time cursing their fate or complaining about those they blame for the situation. Johnny can't read. Undoubtedly someone is to blame, but however emotionally satisfying such activity may be, castigating that someone will not help Johnny. Johnny is here now. He needs help now. If he does not get this help, his entire life will be changed for the worse, as will the life of the nation, for Johnny is not a single isolated student. There are countless Johnnies.

Teaching this fundamental tool—reading—is priority number one. However, it may well take some time, although the amount may vary from pupil to pupil and from situation to situation. Should all other education come to a complete halt while the nonreader tries to catch up? Ideally the answer should be "Yes!" A crash program that would give the student the ability to read rapidly would justify the time lost by virtue of (1) the time saved in dealing later with other (content) subjects because the pupil would then master them faster and with better comprehension, thus making up for the lost time, and (2) the time *not* lost with a futile and unproductive expenditure of energy wasted in trying to master subjects that require the ability to read well. In actuality many students demand instant gratification, and, therefore, will not expend the time and effort to learn to read. It is often an unfortunate fact that those most in need of improvement in a given area, as here, for reading:

(1) do not see the need for mastery of the subject (if they did they would already have worked hard—or harder—at learning it); or

(2) do not believe that they can master it (hence, by their fallacious reasoning, are unwilling to "waste" their time).

Such students often think that they can bypass the subject and, therefore, call for "relevant" courses—relevant, that is, to their immediate objective (presumably a college degree in some specific area). Of course, no single subject can be more relevant to their ultimate needs, regardless of whether or not they themselves are able to perceive this truth. It is an ironic fact that quite often the particular people most willing and even desirous of taking instruction in reading are those who *already* read well—and thus appreciate the advantages that the ability to read rapidly confers—but who want to learn to read even faster and with more comprehension. Nonetheless, since the poor or nonreaders will often drop out of the educational system (or alternatively attack it violently) rather than submit to a (to them) unpleasant, unproductive, ungratifying discipline, and since many college professors, whether from actual conviction or from cynical opportunism, see nothing anomalous in putting nonreaders into classes that require reading skill, it becomes imperative to devise means of continuing to educate the students *even if they can't read.* It goes without saying that the nonreaders must get the specific training they need, either immediately or eventually, but the practical exigencies of even keeping them in school preclude attacking the problem head-on. Therefore, it is necessary to educate these nonreaders—but in a way that takes into account the fact that at the present stage of their development they are incapable of profiting from instruction which is geared to capable readers. Merely to put these nonreaders into the regular classes, as has been done—with ofttimes catastrophic results—is a travesty of schooling: it may satisfy their egos temporarily (usually until they discover that they can't perform adequately), but it does them no favor since they don't learn, and it does do a distinct disservice both to them since they waste their time and, worse yet, form a negative image of themselves and to their classmates, since the level of instruction of the class is necessarily lowered by the presence of students who can't keep up with the work. The problem then is simply one of giving *genuine* instruction to nonreaders.

To a phenomenal degree, most teachers of today have never seriously faced the centrality of this problem. The reasons are manifold. In part, at least, one cause is their inability to grasp the extent to which the need to read pervades our entire culture. Those who have grasped this indisputable fact hesitate to seek the remedy since this cure requires drastic changes and troublesome revision of their well established procedures. Instead, therefore, they seek either to assign the blame (always to someone other than themselves) or to ignore the problem completely in the pious but ill-founded hope that somehow Johnny will increase his reading skill on his own if he is merely assigned enough homework that will force him to read. It should be obvious that, if such assignments have not improved a pupil's reading skill in elementary and high school, still stiffer assignments will not be helpful in college. On the contrary, the nonreader's frustration may well lead him either to drop out of college or, from one point of view, worse yet, to commit violence as his only, inarticulate way of protesting the "system." Furthermore, as suggested, merely assigning the blame cannot help Johnny here and now, although possibly it may preclude the development of future nonreaders who advance beyond their ability to receive instruction from a reading-oriented educational system. Yet one important consideration is often overlooked. There still are societies and through the ages there have been other societies in which no one at all or—in some instances—only a very select group was able to read. Instruction *was* given and received in these societies. It is true that the substance of the instruction usually differed from that given in our own culture. Yet in at least many specific areas the content was no less sophisticated than that of our own system. In early Old Irish times, for example, a professional class of bards used to commit the *entire* body of their literary tradition to memory—word by word—without the aid of writing. Furthermore they lacked many of the auxiliary devices now readily available if our educational system will only make use of them.

To reassert the most pressing need, then, in order to rescue Johnny from the educational scrap heap it is imperative to revise the teaching approach so as to reach him and other nonreaders via media other than print and by means other than the average, often (unfortunately) inadequate teacher. How then can this task be done?

From time to time, even in traditional schools, classes have gone on trips to plays or movies. These departures from the educational norm appear as high points of excitement and interest amidst plateaus of educational boredom. Part of the stimulation undoubtedly arises simply from the breaking of the day-to-day routine. Another important factor (and not one to be underrated), however, is the direct exposure to master artists—writers, directors, actors—who have far more to offer than the harassed teacher does. It is true that no one—*absolutely no one*—can perform on the highest level consistently, without any lulls or dull points. It is also true, nevertheless, that there is no insurmountable reason why such special presentations devised with all of the skill of dedicated professionals cannot occupy a greater proportion of the school day.

The most immediate objection is the wasted motion in time, effort, and money. In order to take a class to see a Broadway play, for example, the teacher has to double as fund raiser (getting the students to beg the money from their parents), lawyer (getting permission, with legal releases for time out from school, not to mention for escape clauses in case of accidents in transit), organizer (making arrangements, plotting the travel route, etc.), and guide (herding the students down to the theater, seeing that all get on the same train, etc.). Even under such adverse conditions, the occasional trips have invariably justified themselves in terms of intellectual joy and awakening. Long after he has graduated and years after he has forgotten most of the daily class lessons, many a former student remembers such a special trip with a pleasurable glow. Many a lifelong interest in—one might even say romance with—the theater started with just such a trip. Yet why must this happiness represent a deviation from the norm rather than the norm itself? Why shouldn't joy be a regular concomitant of a well devised educational program?

Clearly, of course, for a variety of reasons, no school in the world is geared to *daily* trips to the theater. The time lost in going and coming, the supervisory strain on the teachers, the financial strain on the parents all are prohibitive. Yet there is no need for the class to go to the show. Reverse the procedure and bring the presentation to the student—not, of course, the actual Broadway cast in person but the nearest equivalent possible. Most of the great works of literature and many of the major plays originally presented on Broadway have been made into motion pictures. If these films were released to the schools, they could be presented in the school auditoriums to audiences consisting of many class sections at once. The economics of this type of transaction will be discussed later. For the moment, consider the two-fold educational gain:

(1) Students who cannot read or who read poorly could view these works with pleasure.

(2) Students who *can* read well often still profit by the skillful performances and understanding interpretations of talented actors, plus the appropriate visual settings that intensify and make real the works.

It should be obvious that an entire curriculum cannot be built around a steady diet of plays and other purely literary fare, the usual substance of English courses. However history, philosophy, psychology, and many other traditional subjects *can* be presented in this guise. The author of this book remembers to this day a motion picture of the Crusades presented more than thirty years ago. While parts of that movie took artistic liberties for dramatic effect, such details were readily recognized as Hollywood-type embellishments. The major sweep of the picture, though, did portray the historical events with some fidelity. The film did serve to make those medieval events meaningful to a child of twelve. Later advanced reading changed this author's view of the Crusades, but this change represented a matter of interpretation based on additional information. Even the alternative view *could* have been presented in the movie.

Discussions with historians regarding the feasibility of presenting history via motion pictures or videotapes reveal mixed views. Most scholars agree that a good part of history can be presented and learned in this manner. Some historians object, however, that often there are conflicting views. How does one avoid distortion or misrepresentation? The answer, however, is obvious. Just as one can film a dramatic rendition of the historic events, so can one record on film a lively discussion between historians representing rival points of view. A film, in fact, can enliven such a discussion beyond what the actual presence of the scholars themselves would permit. A film could digress to show the documents or other evidence in the original and on the actual sites in which they are found. Furthermore this sort of debate could only be viewed by a small audience if it were not recorded on film. The intensity, the emotion, the excitement of scholars caught up in the exposition of their scholarly findings often disappears when set down dispassionately in colorless, impersonal scholarly prose. The visual record on film or videotape would convey to the audience the liveliness of the issues, with exactly the same wonder as a detective story unfolding itself.

Another objection—a legitimate one—raised by some historians relates to the need for would-be historians to deal directly with source materials. Certainly the use of film is not intended to preclude *all* scholarship based on reading. It only represents a recognition of the hard reality that some students *already in school* can't read. If they are to learn at all, they must imbibe this learning through media that they can handle. Eventually, if—and only if—they advance far enough they will have to acquire the tools of their trade. Obviously the ability to read well is one such tool, perhaps *the* most important one. Yet, even if they can't read, they still can, as indicated, learn both the major facts and even the diversities of opinion about those facts of history. The major point is the continuity of the learning process, pending the acquisition of the tools they do not possess at the moment.

The second advantage in the use of "stored learning"—besides the simple bypassing of the reading process—is the superior presentation gained. Not all teachers are equally good. This fact is self-evident. A recorded presentation could draw on the skills of the master teacher and bypass the less well trained or less talented pedagogue. The curriculum could be devised by the best people in the field. When desirable, the presentation could draw on them or on professional actors. Furthermore, diagrams or complicated charts or pictures can be projected rapidly, with no loss of time such as occurs in the regular classroom. These more effective presentations then, recorded with greater perspective, clarity, and skill, would to a great extent replace the mediocre teacher, but the use of film could do more as well. It could help improve the skills of all the teachers who remain in the system. By virtue of the time used for the filmed offerings, the teachers would no longer have to do as much preparation in order to occupy the regular classroom hours. The films would preempt the bulk of the time. Instead the teacher could focus on the problems of getting the greatest perspective possible and of involving the students in that broader view. The teaching would avoid most of the trivia now characteristic of the school day and would concentrate only on that which is most meaningful and important.

Thus from this point of view the following advantages would result:

(1) fewer actual trained teachers would be required;

(2) the school boards, therefore, could be more selective in hiring only the best scholars, in effect weeding out the misfits and incompetents;

(3) those teachers remaining would have more time for meaningful preparation; and, therefore,

(4) the class hours would be more exciting and satisfying to the students *and* teachers.

In addition, the cost of education would in the long run, though not necessarily immediately, go down. This lowering of the cost would stem from the fact that only a projectionist would be needed for a good part of the day. A projectionist would require neither the advanced educational training that teachers need nor preparation for each day's presentation. The work involved in putting one film rather than another on the machine is the same. Likewise, the film can be shown to a thousand people as easily as to thirty or forty. Only a single man-hour of a projectionist's time would replace the twenty or thirty man-hours expended by as many teachers under the normal setup.

The future of education will undoubtedly be revolutionized by some of the already available technical advances. What is more, some of these developments answer the need of reaching illiterates or poor readers. The video cartridge with any type of material stored and ready for use can be mass produced. At the moment only a few companies are producing serious works geared to educational needs. Once the entire educational system adopts the use of teacher-bypassing presentations such as films or cartridges, these materials will have multimillion-dollar markets. Hence,

(1) large-scale production methods will continue to reduce costs until the price tag is almost negligible, and

(2) full-time staffs, and fully exploited production facilities will be able to call on and afford the most capable educators, writers, performers, technicians, and other personnel to produce the material for educational use. The enormous distribution will prorate the costs of each specialist among millions of consumers. Hence there will be motivation for better productions in a competitive market while at the same time these improved products will be even less expensive.

Since the videotapes will be viewable on home screens, the actual homework may occupy the major portion of school time. Schools can readily distribute the subject cartridges for home viewing—or, alternatively, if the costs are lowered enough, the pupils may purchase them outright and build libraries of cartridges. Thus the actual time spent in school may well be reduced to only a few hours, or a day or two per week. The teachers would in some instances become teachers rather than baby sitters or jailers for the first time.

Since education could be pursued so largely in the home, more people would, one might expect, progress to higher educational levels. Education would become a lifelong process as it should. The discussion of this possibility though is left for a separate chapter. Here let it suffice to note that the new technology may carry within itself the answer to the needs of increasingly open, widespread education.

26. Public Education of the Future

There once was a time when the idea of providing everyone with a free elementary-school education seemed like the zenith of public planning, and, in fact, few individuals went on to the high-school level. Later a high-school education became so much the norm that a secondary-school diploma became a prerequisite for even the most menial job. Now a rising tide of open-admissions policies indicates that in the foreseeable future almost all citizens who want one will acquire a college degree. Evidence presented in this book has suggested that in at least some instances the passage of open admissions as a policy has not always been accompanied by the financial and other implementation necessary to make the political decision a meaningful educational one. Quite the contrary, as demonstrated, the influx of enormous numbers of poorly prepared students into an already overburdened system has created tremendous problems at the college level, thus leading to a frightening decline in the effectiveness of the institutions involved—even for training the well-prepared students, as measured by pre-open-admissions standards.

The threat posed by this irresponsible and somewhat schizophrenic planning, which involves rising expectations and challenges but diminished capacity to fulfill the hopes or meet the needs, led me to define open admissions as "a political device for conferring a college degree without providing a college education." This remark, uttered in a moment of despair, deliberately ironical and cynical, was quoted by Evans and Novak in a column that appeared in over two hundred newspapers throughout the country. The discrepancy between the promise and the reality *is* very real and *must not* be underestimated. To miscalculate or fail to react sharply and effectively could lead, if the most dangerous possibility is realized, to the demise of the entire system of higher education in this country. Yet, in the balance lies the fact that there *always* has been a marked dichotomy between promise and reality. The little red schoolhouse of frontier- or post-frontier-days fame was hardly the ideal educational enterprise. Often a single teacher possessing little more than a high school diploma herself, if even that, had to cope with students at every educational level from kindergarten up, turning from one class level to another, improvising, experimenting, making do without proper textbooks or other aids today regarded as commonplace and even as necessities. Sometimes the overworked teacher employed the more advanced students to help the beginners. By one means or another she muddled through. One may anticipate that by some means or other the present educational system will also "muddle through," and, just as the one-teacher, haphazard-standards enterprise eventally gave way to the modern school system, with the accompanying teams of trained specialists, planning boards, and so on, the present, temporarily disrupted pattern will correct itself, renew standards, and settle down to a more desirable future.

At the moment many educators still actually fear even to discuss standards, lest they be accused of bigotry against minority groups, who often have not done well *(as groups)* by the usual measures. Some still discuss "cultural deprivation" as magic words to explain away the failures of the educational system, and they regard the poor showings of some students on standard tests as evidence that the teachers or the ones who devised the tests are biased. Nevertheless,in closed discussions of committees and planning boards, and in reports of departments, the extreme hypersensitivity, the willful misunderstanding, and the outright cowardice which would dictate a hands-off, no-standards and no-monitoring-or-measuring policy, are beginning to give way to American common sense and practicality. Thus, for example, a graduate committee discusses what kind of support can be provided to a "high-risk" group with a drop-out rate of four out of every five. It discusses means for channeling some students into more realistic paths directed toward goals which they *can* reasonably expect to achieve. It recognizes that it is no kindness—although it may be democratic—to allow students to think that everyone can get a doctorate in any field. The right to try is not the same as the actual ability to master the subject matter. Although membership in a minority group should not disqualify anyone from a desired goal, mere membership in the group is likewise no proper academic qualification for certification in a field. Eventually, of course, realistic considerations *will* override the current ego-based political hypersensitivity, although the length of time nonacademic considerations will rule or the amount of damage that will result inevitably must vary from place to place. Nonetheless, occasional behind-the-scene activity suggests a return to normal, more objective criteria for measuring genuine achievement. Yet what lies beyond a mere return to "normality" in American educational circles?

Today writers on education hail the open-admissions policy at the college level as the new frontier of education. Actual planning groups, on the other hand, fully expect to see a graduate open-admissions policy as well, and undoubtedly this level will be reached. Yet education, both formal and informal, is properly a lifelong activity. People can learn at any age. As they mature, their goals, needs, or aspirations change. As this writer, who has spent an entire lifetime in the educational field, sees the problem, there should be absolutely *no* upper limits on the amount of education made available to anyone with a genuine desire to learn. Even the doctoral degree, now taken as the highest educational mark of achievement, represents only a certification of minimal competence at a given level in some specified field. Courses taken long after I had passed the normal Ph.D. level proved far *more* meaningful than those taken before because the broader background already acquired gave insight into interconnections and potentialities that would have been impossible to grasp without the additional knowledge.

The educational system of the future should be arranged in such a way that anyone who can demonstrate the ability to profit from a course should be allowed, with little or (ideally) no cost, to enroll in that course, provided only that his presence does not disrupt that class or lower the level of achievement of his classmates. Citizens should feel free to drop out of school at any time or at any rung in the academic ladder, confident that they will be allowed to resume their studies whenever they wish.

The modern era is an era of change. Whole industries disappear overnight because of a single legislative decision. New fields spring into existence following a chance technical discovery. Many people make the crucial decision to "major" in a particular field when they are only eighteen or twenty, but then, as a consequence of that decision, remain trapped in the chosen field, which very well may not prove congenial or profitable or desirable to them, for the rest of their lives. Yet how can an eighteen-year-old, with hardly any perspective, anticipate what he or the rest of society will be like twenty years later? Obviously he can't. Nor can anyone else. Certainly, in this age of increasingly longer life spans, no forty-year old ought to suffer for the quarter of a century which remains to his productive working life because of the decisions made earlier by an immature youth.

Schools should be open and free to *anyone* at any age, regardless of how long that individual has been away from academic life. Furthermore, the availability of education should not be tied merely to employment-motivation, although assuredly a strong case can be—and often has been—made that the state actual derives increased revenues when it improves the educational level of its citizenry, as a direct result of the positive correlation between educational attainment and monetary income, hence, eventually, taxes. It is certainly good business practice to promote education.

Yet education is more than a path to earning power. It is the highway to a more vital and meaningful life. There is no reason why a housewife who wants to master the art of cake decoration—or archaeology or paleontology, for that matter—should not have the opportunity to do so. Why shouldn't the grocer with an interest in philosophy or a physician with an urge to paint pursue those impulses? The intent need not be purely utilitarian. Joy and satisfaction are reason enough in themselves, although I can think of many instances where the pursuit of knowledge because of the pleasure it yielded actually led to a vocational change. Thus a truck driver with an interest in the Bible started to take evening courses. After a while, as his fund of knowledge grew, he was called on to address a church congregation from time to time on topics about which he had special competence. He continued to study, with no original objective beyond the happiness it afforded, but eventually he realized that he could make religion his vocation as well as his avocation. When he died a few years ago, he was one of the best loved ministers in Harlem, and the size of the crowd of mourners was a tribute to the understanding and wisdom that can grow out of the pursuit of knowledge for its own sake.

When the inevitable increase in the use of video cassettes (discussed previously) comes into widespread use, this kind of avocational education will be commonplace. More and more people will utilize their leisure time for educational advancement, and the sheer weight of the numbers involved will contribute to an ever higher level of general competence as a result of the fact that people will continue to pursue their studies longer because of the following:

(1) the convenience of being able to stay at home for much of the instruction;

(2) the possibility of dropping out, resuming, and dropping out just as often as they wish, when the mood strikes them; and

(3) the improved presentations of the material in consequence of the response of the producers to the needs of an enormous and highly profitable educational market.

This increase in advanced study among more and more people will mean:

(1) that many more will reach the level now associated with the doctoral degree and, of more far reaching impact,

(2) that still others will go far *beyond* this level, mastering perhaps ancillary and cognate fields to a similar range of competence.

A good many of these people may well remain employed in fields other than that of their new educational pursuits. Such situations will probably not even be rare, let alone unknown. Countless people, already well established in businesses or professions, will widen their interests. The sheer convenience alluded to—of continuing their education under such conditions—may induce them to pursue all of those will-o-the-wisp impulses which now are disregarded as impractical. Once enough people do acquire high *post*-doctoral level competences, a demand for an appropriate degree should emerge, and thus perhaps the creation of a new level in the educational hierarchy—a type of superdoctorate, possibly even more than one. Such advanced degrees will reflect the fact that citizens of the future will be the most well educated people in all history. More than that, holders of these new degrees will be capable of understanding, formulating, and solving a wider range of problems than can now even be envisioned. The advantages that will accrue to society as a whole can hardly be calculated.

27. Teaching in Languages Other Than English: The Crack in the Dam?

A teacher at Benjamin Franklin High School in New York City informed me that she had been having assigned to her, as an instructor in English, classes of students—mainly Spanish-speaking—who knew no English at all. New York City, of course, has long been a port of entry for many immigrant groups, and there has never been any requirement that these newcomers to our land must know English as a prerequisite for admission. In the normal course of events, they and their children would learn enough English to function in a predominantly English-speaking society. However, for a number of reasons irrelevant to the point to be made here—among them, perhaps, the obligatory-promotion policy—many of the students at this high school were being graduated and were receiving diplomas *although they still could speak little or no English.* Now since, as pointed out before, the City University had adopted a monolithic policy of accepting *anyone* with a diploma from a New York City high school, the institution therefore necessarily had to accept these students along with the others.

At a meeting of the Alumni Association the term before the scheduled start of the open-enrollment policy, I directed a query to Dr. Seymour Hyman, the Assistant Chancellor of the City University, regarding the problem posed by the entrance of non-English speakers into the system. Dr. Hyman, taking the question as an attack on open admissions rather than as a simple request for information, grew angry and spoke about "you people who don't want open admissions to succeed."

On being reminded that he hadn't answered the question, he finally said that the university would teach them in Spanish if they didn't know English. Besides, he asserted, there couldn't be too many such students.

"Probably not," came the reply, "but do you mean to say that the university is going to give a Spanish-language version of every single one of the hundreds of courses now in the curriculum? Also, if it does, will it provide the same service for native speakers of languages other than Spanish, say Italian, Yiddish, French, Polish, and so forth?"

Dr. Hyman, alternately shouting and speaking in tones dripping with hostility and sarcasm, asserted that the problem was not a problem at all. No amount of requestioning, however, could force him to come to grips with—or even acknowledge—the problem, although it seemed to me a logical consequence of the policies already formulated. Finally the chairman of the meeting intervened to change the topic.

Despite Dr. Hyman's reaction, part of a head-in-the-sand syndrome endemic among certain supposedly liberal educators who do not have answers to consequences often enough of their own devising, the problem remains. In fact, it is being pushed back one stage. Certain groups in New York, with the crusading support of at least one politician, have been quite justifiably pointing to the number of dropouts among the high school students who understand *only* Spanish and no English. Obviously such students are incapable of profiting from instruction given in a tongue they cannot comprehend. Thus, bored and frustrated, they escape at the earliest moment possible from an educational situation which to them is intolerable. When legally forced to remain in school, they cut classes when they are able and, often enough, disrupt classes when they are not.

The problem, whether set in the City University or in the elementary or high school (and whether in New York City or elsewhere), is a real problem. Political pressures are now pushing for a two-track —English-speaking and Spanish-speaking—system. The New York problem is two-fold: a short-term and a long-term one. The most immediate consideration is that of whether or not the city can afford to duplicate all courses. After all, the need is not just for one or two sections of a single course. The students need to go through an entire curriculum, extending through the normal period of school years. Just as obviously, at the present moment, the city, which is cutting back on its personnel list wherever feasible, can most assuredly not undertake an enormous addition to its overtaxed resources.

The long-term consideration is that which takes into account not the consequences to the city of the decision, but rather the consequences to the students. Although instruction given in Spanish *might* reduce the drop-out rate, such a solution would diminish the likelihood of the students ever learning English. In an English-speaking society such a limitation would also lessen the students' chances for successful careers in any of a large number of fields. One could argue —and it has been argued—that New York City may eventually become largely Spanish-speaking, but even if this surmise—a guess at best—were accurate, the students then would be limited to Spanish-speaking areas of the country. They would lack entry into most of the country. Consequently, any move to give the students instruction in their native language would constitute a disservice, not a service, to them.* Despite the long-term consideration, however, the practical fiscal limitation rules out a two- or multitrack system, even without augmenting the cost still further by adding instruction in additional languages for those whose native tongue is neither English nor Spanish.

As seen, whether encountered in the grammar schools, because of the disruptions or dropouts, or in the university, because of the

*I not only see no objection in offering selected substantive courses in a foreign language, but view such possibilities as desirable, since they would enable many foreign-born students to retain their language skills. Such courses, however, should not be handled, or allowed to be utilized, as the means to avoid mastering English. They would be additions to, not substitutions for, the regular curriculum.

consequences of the simplex open-admissions policy, the problem *must* be faced at some level, sooner or later. That answer, however, lies not in denying the existence of the situation but rather in the appropriate educational innovation and the proper (and sophisticated) use of already available resources. The teaching of English to a speaker of Spanish (or Polish or whatever) differs in no fundamental way from the reverse situation, teaching a foreign languge to a native speaker of English. The only superficial distinction—more apparent than real—lies in the urgency of the situation. Spanish speakers cannot function at all in classrooms where English is the language of instruction, at least not until they have progressed in their English-speaking and English-comprehending ability. A later chapter deals with the need for drastic changes in the organization of foreign-language instruction. Therefore the matter of intensive English-language training for those to whom that language is strange will be deferred. In my opinion the problem is easily solved. However, it must be solved by actually dealing with it, not by pretending it doesn't exist! Some educators such as those (many at least) of the City University make decisions out of political motivations (i.e., open admissions as an exciting experiment in social engineering) but then refuse to deal *at the educational level* with the consequences of those decisions. Furthermore, as seen here from Dr. Hyman's reaction, they impute to those who raise relevant questions about difficulties arising from those same decisions sinister motivations rather than a simple and hard-headed recognition of the need to deal with reality—with what is, rather than what they would like to be. Because of the paranoid fears of some of those operating from political motivations, their own goals (which very well may be, and often are, shared by others) must be brought into the realm of the achievable by genuine educators over *the resistance of the pseudo-educators.* Clearly, as suggested here, any multitrack system would engender disaster to those whom it purports to help as well as to all the others who would suffer because of the fantastic drain on the fiscal resources.

28. Language Study: Total Immersion

Careful consideration and persistent probing reveals that many individuals who label language study as "irrelevant" give (presumably) good reasons—mere justifications—but not the *real* reasons for their antipathy. At bottom they have a deep-seated fear or distaste of tedious, hard work with uncertain return. Occasionally they see the rewards for the effort expended as so chronologically remote that they would rather focus their energy on more immediately gratifying pursuits. A few individuals even confess to an inability to learn a language readily. Unfortunately it is true that by the methods now used, employed at the snail's pace of perhaps three academic hours a week, at least three or four years must elapse before the student can begin to struggle through foreign-language material whose substance is high enough above the "run-Spot-run" level to provide intellectual satisfaction.

If one could promise the student that he would be speaking, reading, and writing with great fluency within *five weeks,* the charge of irrelevancy would disappear overnight. Yet such a promise can be made if one is willing to bypass the traditional academic calendar and the traditional teaching approach. The major difference can be summed up in two words: *total immersion.* The student must devote all of his waking hours of every day for the five-week period focusing solely on the one target language. He must plan his daily menu in the desired language, describe his daily activities in it, even exchange the idle pleasantries of his recreational hours in it. Such an approach and such a schedule worked well for the United States Army during World War II and has continued to work for the State Department, which maintains a special school for career personnel who need to acquire the language of the country to which they are assigned. In the specified time they acquire near-native proficiency. Furthermore there is no question of slow learners or *non*learners. Everyone who speaks his own language has already demonstrated his capacity to learn new languages. When he came into the world, that which was *later* to become his native language was, by and large, unknown to him.* He had to learn it from scratch.

To be sure, an all-day-long devotion to a single subject does not fit the regular academic calendar, but surely the promise of successful mastery of a foreign language to a level that is useful warrants a departure from the rigid academic lock-step. The method—initially oral-aural in presentation—does not need research or investigation to see if it works. It *has worked* for about a quarter of a century. Texts and records have been developed and are readily available.

Why has it not been regularly adopted everywhere? Ignorance, perhaps. Possibly inertia. Probably a fundamental reluctance to depart from the usual school-system scheduling, whereby so many hours a day are devoted to subject one, so many to subject two, and so on. Administrators maintain a democratic impartiality in adjudicating the demands of competing departments and subjects. They are hesitant about allocating the entire "pie" to one course, rather than cutting that pastry into little slices.

Yet the true educational measure is not the day-by-day measure, however ladled out, but rather the total achievement in learning. Instead of a uniform—administratively convenient—term of fifteen weeks geared to a periodic recording of grades at the end of each

*Dr. Henry Truby of the Florida Communications Research Laboratories has disclosed the likelihood that language learning of some sort starts even before birth. The auditory apparatus of the unborn fetus becomes operative long before birth, and the fetus hears much of what takes place to or around the mother via transmission of sound through the abdominal wall. Thus the infant hearing only a particular language spoken starts to sort out the phonemes (or distinctive sound units) of that language so that later he will be more ready to reject accidental productions of sounds which are not meaningful in the language.

prearranged juncture, some flexibility affords sizable advantages in bringing the rewards of learning closer to the time of the learning effort, hence the positive feedback in satisfaction. Likewise much of the wasteful trivia, attendance-taking, repetition of work covered, and so forth is eliminated with salubrious results.

Once the language has been mastered to a high degree of competence, the skills can be maintained and enhanced by the more normal coursework, but this time at a more advanced level, one that can afford pleasure not boredom. Even the greatest literary works of all time lose their appeal when imbibed at the rate of twenty lines a period, three times a week. By acquiring high competence rapidly, the student can proceed to a reading of the great masterpieces composed in the target language *as literature,* not as tedious lessons in grammar or as vocabulary to be learned.

29. Supplementation, Not Remediation

Underlying much of the thinking about the placement of many students is a misguided focus on remediation rather than supplemental or supportive work—the provision of pre- or corequisites. Endemic to this approach is an often unwarranted value judgment about the mentality of the students. All too frequently, because of poor counseling, a pupil weak in mathematics is assigned to a chemistry or physics course which requires a firm background in math. Inevitably the student fails. Sometimes he is made to repeat the course, with—predictably—the same result. The pattern of failure starts to leave a mark—a failure mentality—on the student until he eventually ceases trying, firmly convinced that he just doesn't have what it takes.

The educator reviewing the student's record of failure is likely to agree—to assume a mental deficiency on the part of the student. Yet the weakness in the pupil's mathematical background stems not from his incapacity to do the work or to solve the problems but from the fact that he has never been exposed to the relevant topics. Thus, for example, one girl who wanted to become a nurse was repeatedly steered away from any college preparatory work by a stubborn guidance counselor who, knowing or guessing the girl's poor economic circumstances, assumed that the young lady would be forced to go directly to work after high school graduation. Therefore she put the girl into elementary business arithmetic and secretarial courses instead of the algebra that the would-be nurse needed.

The girl did manage to get herself assigned to a chemistry course, despite her lack of background. When she failed, not once but three times, she saw herself as a subnormal mentality. She never realized that she had been foredestined to failure because she had not had the appropriate prerequisites. Nothing was wrong with her mind. In fact, she was a brighter-than-average student. Eventually she did pursue a business career, but she retained a lifelong sense of failure and frustration. Yet the nation desperately needed and still needs trained nurses, and this girl could have qualified if she had been properly guided.

Not all failure of this type stems from poor planning. Sometimes administrative expediency or educational restructuring plays a role. In one instance a school of nursing availed itself of the chemistry courses given at the associated college of liberal arts and sciences. The intent was a saving of the money necessary for an extra instructor. As with the previous example, the girls did not have enough math to succeed in the same class with science majors. Fortunately an alert departmental chairman became aware of the problem very promptly, and he devised a special three-term sequence to replace the usual two terms. The extra time allowed by the revised sequence, which carried the same college credit allotment (here eight credits), enabled the teacher to give the mathematics the girls lacked. The innovation, perhaps, could not have been instituted at all if just the nursing students had been involved (after all, the girls were really attached to another school, and their admission to the course had been an academic courtesy to a sister institution), but the three-term chemistry sequence filled a definite need for many premedical and predental students as well as for former liberal-arts majors who lacked the mathematics background, but nevertheless had switched over to a science major.

In a similar fashion students without pre- or corequisites in other subjects are sent on to certain failure despite their intellectual ability to succeed if given the right background. Too many of the open-admissions students now being offered an additional chance have already started down the path to failure mentalities because of this inadequate planning. Once such students become convinced of their own inability, unfortunately, they may go through the motions of enrolling for courses, but they do not expend the same alert, intense effort on their work as they would have if they expected success. Ideally, the downward cycle should be caught and corrected before it begins, presumably in the elementary or high school. Pragmatically the colleges have to accept the students wherever they are in their training. One major deficit of this kind occurs among students who have been raised among speakers of foreign languages or of nonstandard dialects of English. The books are written and the lectures and classwork are normally conducted in the preferred prestige-standard dialect of English. Obviously students who don't know English at all are at a disadvantage when placed in classes with native speakers. It is not so widely recognized how the speakers of nonstandard dialects also labor under severe handicaps. This problem deserves extended and, in part, highly specialized discussion. Let it suffice here merely to place this language deficiency in the same class with deficiencies in any other prerequisite. Failure on the part of educators and teachers to recognize and deal with background omissions paves the way for the failure of students—but not merely for the failure in specific courses. The failures initiate a psychological cycle that ends with frustration, boredom, and often hostility to all education. Learning is—and should remain—one of the greatest joys and satisfactions available to human beings. Administrative insufficiency should never deprive our students of that reward.

30. Respice, Adspice, Prospice*

Page one of the *New York Times* of March 13, 1972, quoted a University of Wisconsin senior as saying, "No question about it . . . I never go to school anymore, and I still get wonderful grades." When I mentioned this citation to colleagues from various academic institutions, every single one, without exception, merely shrugged and replied with some equivalent of "So? What's new? Everyone knows that standards have gone down. We don't need newspaper corroboration of what we know for a fact."

Nevertheless, publicly at least, many other academicians—both professors and more especially administrators—make statements extolling the high standards of their own institutions. At a debate between Dr. Robert Marshak, the President of City College of New York, and Professor Howard Adelson, of the same institution, Professor—now (predictably?) Dean—Phillip Baumel jumped up excitedly to interrupt the discussion. Dr. Marshak had already conceded that more than half of the incoming students required remedial work in both English and mathematics, and Professor Adelson had asserted that standards had gone down irretrievably. Professor Baumel proclaimed, as though in triumphal rebuttal, "But the average grades are now higher than they ever were before!"

*"Look back, look to the present, look ahead" (the Latin motto of City College of New York).

Imagine, more than half the students requiring remediation, but the grades being higher than ever. What does that combination imply about the current grading system?

At Clark University in Worcester, Massachusetts, the enrollment for Professor Stanton's Sociology-in-a-Nutshell course numbered over a hundred students, far more than the normal enrollment of an average college course. Why not? Professor Stanton had announced in advance that his pupils would grade themselves. After the term, some questions were raised when approximately ninety percent of the class received As, and about ten percent, Bs. Investigation revealed that twenty-seven students had actually signed up for another course that ran at exactly the same time as this one, hence they could not have been present at all. Doubtless some of this group had had a twinge of conscience when choosing their own grades. Since they had not really taken the course, they did not consider themselves worthy of an A, and therefore took only a B, a grade that had once signified above-average work (the A having been reserved for *superior* accomplishment). This example, one must confess, is extreme and not entirely typical of what is going on in academia. Yet it does not conflict with the general trend of what the sociologist David Riesman has called "grade inflation."

More significant, of course, then the marks, which after all are no more than an inaccurate reflection—a barometer—of the academic substance, is the reality of what goes on in the present-day classrooms. One teacher denied tenure at City College put up a vigorous defense, aided and abetted by many supporters, who pointed to the teacher's popularity with the students. A campus newspaper reported that this instructor would enter his classroom with no lesson plan at all in mind and ask the students what they wanted to discuss for the day. After employing (wasting?) ten or fifteen minutes of the fifty-minute period in choosing a topic, they would then have a "rap session"—more of a coffee klatsch than a program of serious instruction. Again, one must regard this example as atypical and merely suggestive of the unscholarly climate that pervades the universities today. One can, however, discern a far less subjective measure in certain significant shifts that have taken place in the personnel distribution at City College of New York. There, one hundred and five sections of remedial English had to be planned for the Winter semester of 1971. When the director of the remedial English program failed to appear at one meeting of the Curriculum and Teaching Committee, the dean of the college commented, "Mina's in a state of shock. She just saw the figures on the number of remedial students we'll be getting." During that same academic year (which included the Spring semester of 1972), mathematics and even physics instructors had to be switched away from the teaching of their regular college-level courses to remedial mathematics. New teachers were hired where possible for this purpose. At the same time or perhaps shortly thereafter, because of the budget squeeze, a freeze was imposed on the hiring of personnel. If a scholar resigned, retired, or went on leave, his department was not allowed to obtain someone to take his place. Thus a new and utterly unprecedented weight was necessarily being given to remedial—or properly *pre*-college—work while attrition was taking place in the real college-level teaching staff, thus requiring the obligatory dropping of many courses. The college was shifting to a pre-college institution (a remedial *college?*), one which still bore the old title but which in fact was less than it had been. Again it must be emphasized here that there is nothing wrong or improper in an attempt by an educational institution to educate students who require additional help. What is improper, however, is the fraud implicit in overt and covert attempts to suggest that the level of work at the institution is as high as (or higher than) before. The attrition, then, quite apart from the direct cutting at all levels, even had a chain-reactive effect. Thus, by previous practice, an undergraduate professor asked to teach in a graduate program would normally be replaced by someone hired with funds assigned from the graduate budget. Now, although the payroll office still allocated these graduate-level funds to the undergraduate college, the administrators would not redistribute these to the department which had assigned the professor to the higher teaching post. Hence such departments faced a quandary: either (1) to lose additional courses at the undergraduate level or (2) to refuse to allow their personnel to teach in the graduate program. In the former instance the undergraduate program lost; in the latter, the graduate program. Yet, as late as June of 1972, when presumably all regular hiring of faculty remained frozen, the *New York Times* bore an advertisement seeking "qualified remedial and freshman english (sic) teachers for a special program within the City University."

The world of academia is a relatively small one, despite the hundreds of institutions throughout the country. It forms a closed, interrelated structure, and, when something happens in one quarter, all other sectors feel the effect in one way or another. Thus, when violence proved effective at Berkeley, this successful attempt gave impetus to a similar effort at destroying Columbia University three thousand miles—a whole continent—away. Other disruptions elsewhere broke out in short order after these.

When, in the wake of violence, the City University of New York initiated the open-admissions program, here too the effects were far reaching, both internally *and* externally. The internal effects (standards, atmosphere, focus, etc.) have received attention in the foregoing pages. The external effects still remain subject to debate, with at least some groups such as the Regents Advisory Council, chaired by former Mayor Robert F. Wagner, trying to downgrade the negative impact (one suspects so as to maintain support for open-admissions). Yet even this latter group has acknowledged some fiscal disadvantage to "L.I.U.-Brooklyn, St. John's and Pace." Other observers have attributed to open admissions at least part of the financial failure of New York University, which has announced the closing of its Bronx campus, presumably because of a (predictable) shifting of some students away from that private institution and to the free City University. Columbia, too, undoubtedly has suffered some fiscal loss because of the recent public policy. It is difficult—and perhaps premature—to attempt to assess the *relative* amount of impact which the open-admissions program has had on the private institutions that have clearly suffered financially from a variety of causes—among these the violence which caused direct damage that had to be repaired at great expense, the need to strengthen the campus security forces, the rise in insurance rates, the rejection of governmental programs (i.e., ROTC, various research projects, etc.) that had previously helped financially, and so forth—but certainly the additional loss, large or small, caused by the competition of a tuition-free, tax-supported university cannot be entirely discounted in the total picture of institutions teetering on or near the brink of fiscal disaster. In the period since the council's study, other New York City institutions such as Pratt have announced forthcoming retrenchments, with indications of still worse possibilities in the offing. In the meantime, the City University itself, overtaxed beyond its resources in money, personnel, and space, is being forced to cut back, and it cannot readily take over or replace many of the programs of those private institutions slowly sinking under the weight of too many adverse pressures and burdens. Some factors, such as inflation, assuredly lie beyond the control of academicians to rectify. Yet some institutions could still weather these uncontrollable variables if they did not also have to face the other problems.

Where then does academia stand, and what are its present and future prospects and needs? Clearly many of the factors touched on in this book—the militancy, the deliberate violence, the faculty and administrative duplicity, cowardice, opportunism, and mental laziness, as well as the host of problems that pervade society as a whole—have combined to threaten the very existence of our entire system of higher education, that is, its existence as a genuine academic enterprise, not as a fradulent pretense of a reality that no longer exists. In some instances, to be sure, even the semblance must disappear since some institutions may well fail completely, and from all indications a great many institutions have already reached the extreme limits of their resources. It will take very little additional trouble to force them to close for good. Once they do, the nation is in serious trouble since it relies so heavily on its college-educated citizens for services in a variety of fields. Furthermore, the graduate institutions that form part of the university complexes could not exist, for the most part, without the undergraduate bases because of the relatively higher costs of postgraduate work. Yet once these undergraduates disappear, so will the graduate schools, America's main source of advanced thinkers—those with master- and doctoral-level training.

Folk expectation to the contrary, academicians, by and large, possess no profound wisdom: they are merely highly trained technicians knowledgeable in their own fields, but, with few exceptions, not particularly astute in areas beyond their own spheres of expertise. Furthermore, not too many university professors possess any unusual qualities of physical or moral courage, such as that necessary either to stand up to the pressures I have described—or even to support in less direct ways the efforts of those rare colleagues of theirs who have dared to place their own lives and careers on the firing line so as to stem the tide of anarchy and revolutionary destruction. Likewise, academia has its own share of rascals, opportunists, and others with dubious codes of ethics. How justified was the anguished lament of one student who wanted to reopen the college and get back to class. After watching the faculty in City College's Great Hall debate the crisis for hour after weary hour, digressing and fencing over fine points of parliamentary procedure and usage, but always deliberately skirting the substantive issues, never facing the problems directly or boldly, he finally rose, and, with tears in his eyes and a voice almost choked with emotion, sobbed, "You're all frauds! All my life I've respected you, my professors. I always took everything you ever had to say seriously, but now I see that all you're good for is debate and nit-picking. You're full of talk and hot air, but what have you done to open the college again? Nothing at all, but talk. You express yourselves beautifully. You know all of the platitudes, but what have you really done? Nothing at all! You always see both sides of every question, and you can give all of the references and citations—but you're incapable of reaching a single real decision. You're all paper tigers! I'll never listen to you again. You don't deserve respect."

Unfortunately, with the rare exceptions suggested, his charges were true. Academia in crisis is highly unlikely ever to be saved by the main body of college professors, although there are courageous, clear thinking, and dedicated faculty amidst the others. Likewise many scholars who have repeatedly failed on other fronts—those in particular areas requiring bravery or moral fortitude—nevertheless sometimes come through with useful insights or practical suggestions. Also, many faculty members working behind the scenes sometimes by persistence or endurance manage to raise standards a notch or restore some semblance of reason to one or another sector of academic life. Yet the salvation of the educational system, if it is to come, must come neither from the faculty alone and most assuredly not from the students but rather, fundamentally, from the administration. As illustrated throughout this book, the disastrous failures have stemmed mainly from administrative blindness or cowardice. Most administrators of today have failed to grasp the changed ground rules. They have either missed the distinction between the stipulated goals and the real goals of the revolutionaries or, having comprehended this distinction, have failed to act on the basis of that knowledge, preferring to try to buy off the enemy rather than to deal with it directly.

The new administrator then will have to be firm but just. He will have to be ready for criticism regardless of what he does, yet be prepared to act on the basis of the long- as well as short-term needs of his school. He has to be a person of vision, with plans for the future. He must also be ready to innovate, but not simply for the sake of novelty. Some changes such as the time-restructuring suggested for the rapid teaching of foreign languages (including English for nonspeakers) require no new technology, but only a sensible use of what is already established so as to solve a problem (e.g., the boredom inherent in the undue postponement of the rewards of language learning). Other possible innovations, such as the temporary bypassing of the reading skills, so as to allow education to proceed while these skills are acquired, may rely upon modern inventions (i.e., motion pictures, closed-circuit television, programmed learning, computers, etc.) unavailable and even undreamed of in previous centuries. Still other innovations, such as the presentation in the same course of the prerequisites with the target subjects (e.g., the chemistry courses stretched out with the addition of the necessary mathematics), may merely require an accurate appraisal of the problem itself, together with a willingness to allocate more time and personnel to the problem *before* militancy and violence engendered of frustration erupt and before the would-be students develop failure mentalities.

Certainly the changed conditions require that the education of the future be vastly different from that of the past. Furthermore these changes should be for the better. More people today expect more than ever before. Our capacities also allow us to accomplish more. Beyond presenting a few suggestions and observations in the last few chapters, this book has made no attempt to provide a full blueprint for the system of the future. Here and there experiments are already in progress, or else the hypotheses on which they have been based have passed beyond the experimental stage and are now coming into the realm of known and approved practices. For example, in England a full-scale open-university program (not open admissions, but rather an extensive correspondence program supplemented by televised instruction and by brief periods of residency) now promises hopeful results. This change and others presage some of the potentialities for the future.

The goal of this book has been the presentation and clarification of the issues. I have often observed that *the* major step in finding a solution to any riddle normally is an identification and precise pinpointing of the problem. As suggested then, two separate kinds of problems face our universities and colleges today: those arising naturally and those created deliberately with destructive intent. If, in the long run, the administrators learn to differentiate the two, and to act on that knowledge, neither type should prove impossible or even very difficult to solve.

31. Epilogue

There are some academicans who, for various reasons—not all of them praiseworthy—would deny the seriousness of the situation, asserting, in effect, that there never has been any problem. Their attitude calls to mind the willful blindness of the good citizens of Germany toward the threat of the Nazi party in the early 1930s or that of the Jewish community of Poland and Germany of the same period when far-sighted leaders such as Ze'ev Jabotinsky warned it of the holocaust to come. The mass graves of six and a half million dead remain as memorials to their mistake. Still other academicians acknowledge the problems of the recent past but claim that, after all, violence has subsided in the past year, that with the winding-down of the Vietnamese conflict youthful belligerence on campus has decreased, that, to a great extent SDS and other revolutionary groups have been discredited. To reply, one need only point to incidents—perhaps sieges would be a better word—such as the seizure of buildings on the Columbia University campus in the Spring of 1972. The militant student groups, the revolution-minded faculty, and the outside *agents provocateurs* remain, ready at all times to utilize local dissatisfaction or even pretexts to stir up trouble. They stand ready to employ to the utmost any opportunities for disaffection. Instigators such as Rennie Davis still remain, prepared to fly, if need be, to wherever they can perform their deliberate and carefully thought-out task—the destruction of the American system of higher education.

What may stand on the positive side of the ledger are the occasional, tantalizingly brief, glimpses of a return to sanity here and there: the decision at Stanford to dismiss Bruce Franklin, the student groups which have sued in the law courts to force vacillating administrators to safeguard the rights of nondisruptive as well as disruptive students, and so on. Having in mind the shameful history of academia's inaction and endless futile debate in the face of destruction, coercion, and blackmail, many students and their parents have become increasingly unwilling to wait for the academics to do what is properly their job. Consequently such groups realistically act on their own behalf, forcing the academics to face the facts and to act, rather than to posture while pretending to see all sides of every question—yet, in effect, giving away the rights of those least likely to vent any hostility on them. The trials by fire have stripped away some of the pretenses and masks of academia. Likewise on the positive side, although hardly deserved, is the grant of additional millions of dollars voted by Congress to prevent the complete fiscal collapse of many faltering institutions. Yet the same issues of newspapers that announced the financial windfall also carried the report of the Carnegie Foundation on Higher Education, warning that academia would have to trim its budget by about twenty percent in the near future or face disaster. This report included an assumption that federal and other sources would add an extra sixteen billion dollars to make up a still-remaining deficit after such a cut.

Clearly, beyond the violence and its immediate consequences, the American higher educational system faces many serious threats. The affirmative-action program, vigorously and stupidly pursued in the name of equality, threatens standards already eroded to a devastating degree.* The consequences of the decisions made under duress (i.e.,

*After this book was already in proof, the author received a memorandum from an associate dean of a prominent medical school to an official of the Association of Medical Colleges, on the subject of "Legal Considerations Related to Minority Group Recruitment and Admissions." The note, based on a consultation with five New York State Supreme Justices, who asked—with good reason—"to remain anonymous," stated that "establishing percentages or quotas of minority students to be accepted in a class represents predictable problems. This should be avoided at all costs. *It is possible to achieve the same results without giving the appearance of restricting portions of the class for designated groups.*" Thus an entire group of medical schools was moving in the direction of quotas while, for legal reasons, pretending that the quotas weren't really quotas.

the acceptance under open admissions of poorly prepared students) still remain to be overcome or somehow minimized. As suggested, once—and if—the problems are faced squarely and honestly, they can be handled. Despite my harsh negative criticisms of the faculty and administrators of so many of today's institutions of higher learning, there nevertheless remains a vast pool of intellect and resourcefulness—which *can* serve to rectify the current situation. I believe that there is no one—no one at all—who cannot be taught effectively and efficiently by the appropriate methods. However, the problems must be brought into the open so that genuine educators—not the cowardly frauds directing or teaching at some of the institutions—may have a fair chance to bring to bear their best capabilities. The American system of higher education may be down at the moment—but it need not remain there.

APPENDICES

Appendix I

Memorandum Distributed to the City College Faculty Council (Chapter 9)

To the Faculty Council:

Under the concept of open admissions we are no longer permitted to require high school preparation in terms of required subject matter entrance units or any form of curricular balance. Likewise we are not permitted to insist that the student remove entrance deficiencies since by definition there are no entrance deficiencies, if only for the reason that there are no mandated entrance units. Thus unless the Faculty Council wishes to introduce controls in the form of degree requirements we shall in subsequent years be granting the B.A. degree to students who in some instances have not had any exposure to a foreign language and who furthermore have never been introduced to any form of mathematics beyond simple arithmetic. With respect to the B.S. candidate the mathematics requirement is self enforcing since all B.S. candidates are required as part of their degree prescriptions to complete a year of calculus. The B.S. student, however, could readily escape an acquaintanceship with a foreign language.

I shall not belabor the other three traditional entrance requirements (4 years of English, 1 year of American history and 1 year of science). These former requirements are in large measure self enforcing. For example, all B.A. and B.S. candidates must pass a proficiency test in written English as part of their degree requirements. With respect to history it is the rare student who has not completed American history and several terms of social science in high school. Our introductory science courses in the college are not built upon high school courses. Furthermore division A of the CORE requirements mandates a minimum of one course in laboratory science for B.A. students.

When our curriculum was drastically modified two years ago the Faculty Council probably assumed—if indeed it gave any thought to the matter at the time—that our entering freshmen would continue to present for admission three years of a foreign language and a mathematics sequence that carried the student through at least intermediate algebra and that the deficiencies, if any, would have to be removed during the early part of the college course of study. During the past two years we have assumed this to be the correct interpretation and have proceeded accordingly.

Under the open admissions concept of curriculum we can proceed in either of the two following directions:

1. We can take the position that the B.A. degree can be granted without any exposure to mathematics beyond grade school arithmetic and that both the B.A. and B.S. degrees can be conferred without exposure to any language other than English.

or alternatively

2. We can require all B.A. students to complete mathematics through at least intermediate algebra (either in high school or college or any combination thereof) and require both B.A. and B.S. students to complete the study of a foreign language for three years or the equivalent either in high school or college or any combination thereof (in college a semester of foreign language is normally considered to be the equivalent of a year in high school).

The Faculty Council should take action on this problem before open admissions becomes a reality in September 1970.

Robert L. Taylor
April 9, 1970

Appendix II

Memorandum Distributed to the Committee on Curriculum and Teaching (Chapter 9)

THE CITY COLLEGE
NEW YORK, N.Y.

April 14, 1970

TO: Members of the Committee on Curriculum & Teaching
FROM: Gabriella de Beer
SUBJECT: Degree Requirements for B.A. and B.S. Students

Based on the enclosed memorandum, the following motion was passed unanimously at the meeting of the Faculty Council on April 9, 1970.

> All B.A. students are required to complete mathematics through at least plane geometry (either in high school or college or any combination thereof) and both B.A. and B.S. students are required to complete the study of a single foreign language for three years or the equivalent either in high school or college or any combination thereof (in college a semester of foreign language is normally considered to be the equivalent of a year in high school).

The Mathematics Department will be offering courses in elementary algebra and plane geometry on a non-credit basis. However, since language courses are credit-bearing, the Faculty Council referred to this committee the matter of whether language courses taken by students who have never had any in high school should count toward division "B" of the distribution requirement.

Appendix III

Characteristic Notices of the Kind Posted on Campus Almost Daily

Hate-America advocates plastered copies of the following notice about every two feet along the corridor walls of Mott Hall and of other City College of New York buildings. Apart from the inaccuracy of the charges, (1) the sheet misspelled the names not only of some of the "prot-fascist (sic) scum" but even that of Professor Gadol, a leading campus radical, and (2) the compiler of the sheet, presumably the C. Axios listed on the opposite side next to the label "Nat'l Caucus of Labor Committee'—an individual actually identifiable by means of another notice (not given) as a member of the Greek Communist Party, had failed to observe that one of the professors accused was not even in the country at the time and had not been for nearly a year.

The unscrupulous nature of their tactics appears in the fact that the "Prof. H. Pachter—Pol. Sci. Dept.," listed with Axios in a manner suggesting that he too was going to speak on "Fascism: The Final Stage of Capitalism," actually opposed the premise. Professor Pachter, a very distinguished scholar whose name the Communists were thus misusing, was scheduled to debate with Axios. The poster *should* have read "Axios (pro) *vs.* Pachter (contra)."

Such notices—and others exhorting to outright revolution—appeared regularly.

FASCISM

The Final Stage of Capitalism

C. Axios - nat'l Caucus of Labor Committee

Prof. H. Pachter - Pol. Sci. Dept. CCNY

March 2 - 12-2 PM

Finley 328

sponsored by
National Caucus of Labor Committees

Fascism: The Final Stage

As the political and economic crisis of capitalism deepens, certain sections of the U.S. capitalist class, see the only solution for continued capitalist "stability" in fascism. More enlightened (sic) sections of that class are seeing Phase II remedies rapidly playing out their usefulness; no, this crisis will not be solved by merely stringent parliamentary economic and political measures.

To the future Hitlers, Speers and Krupps of the U.S. this crisis will be solved by that historically specific form of capitalist rule -- fascism. In this context, the NCLC has already done an admirable job of both exposing and encountering in political debate, two necessary parts of a future fascist political movement.

It was in his Dec. 2 debate with the Labor Committees that Abel Lerner, "neutral" academician and prominent Keynesian economist at Queens College, displayed his fond affinity for the economic policies of Hjalman Schact, Hitler's own economic economic minister. What is more, these policies of stringent wage austerity cloosely pursued by the Nazis in Germany, are the very same policies being offered by Lerner for consideration on capitalist drawing boards!

The University Center for Rational Alternatives, the organization headed by Lerner and the heinously reactionary Sidney Hook (including in its membership CCNY Professors. H. Adelson, M. Ettenberg, L. Gardner, L. Heller, M. Kraus, W. Moslow, G. Sukin, and H. Villard), is now and will in the future demonstrate its competence as future fascist material. Its attempted witchhunts of campus radicals (City's Prof. Gardol), its role in the Angela Davis and Bruce Franklin cases, and in general, its campus HUAC nature make it an essential component of a future right-wing extra-legal political movement. These prot-fascist scum are now posturing as neutral and properly academic while in effect, they are giving the ideological and political justification for an assault on the living standards of working people. To more desperate layers of the capitalist class, the increasing political importance of these currents as a sledge-hammer against the working class will be bared.

It is imperative that fascism be both understood historically and in its present day reality. This can be begun through the exposure of UCRA and other proto-fascist political currents. By necessity, this campaign is taking place in the pages of our newspaper, New Solidarity and in scheduled public forums and debates.

Kill Pigs Dig Dope Kill Pigs Dig Fucking Kill Pigs Dig Yourself Kill Pigs

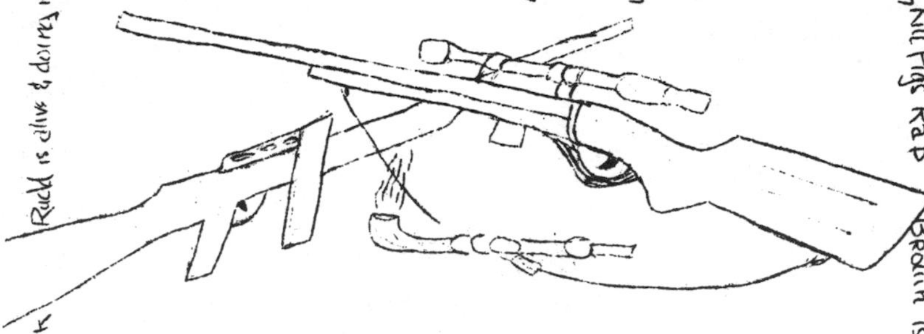

WE'RE ALL STILL ALIVE AND WELL AND DOING IT!! .... Remember Rap Brown? Pat Swinton? Kathy Boudin? Pun Plimondon? They didn't go underground to hide--shit, man, they went under so they could keep blowin' things up. Keep living and being with people. The underground isn't a life of dark cellars and back alleys--it's a new name and a face, it's walkin' in the sun, tripping, fucking, moving offensively against Amerika. It's sniping at pigs in Harlem, brlowing up pig stations in Berkeley, firebombs at Judge Murtaugh's house, higacking an ammo ship to Cambodia. We mean death to Racist Pig Amerika! Life and victory to the people of the world. The Cong, Al Fatah and others are killing Amerika from the outside. We can do it inside. All you need is a group of friends and a little knowledge... then power is ours!!

— tampax fuse (of rag), soaked with lighter fluid, gas

—2/3 gas, 1/3 oil (soapflakes for thickening)

MOLOTOV COCKTAIL

light fuse and throw-- on breaking, contents will ignite:

to throw through windows broken with rocks (pig stations, draft boards, factories, research centers)

SPONTANEOUS COMBUSTION:

Moisten rags with a mixx of 30% turpentine and 70% linseed oil. To ignite pour on any commercial paint dryer. Fire starts as dryer evaporates.

to leave in office and store trash cans, pockets in clothes in department stores, etc. ...

Kill Pigs Rap Brown is alive & doing it Cathy Wilkerson is alive & doing it Kill Pigs Pun Plimondon is alive & doing it Kathy Boudin is alive & doing it

Kill Pigs Pat Swinton is alive & doing it Eldridge is alive & doing it Mark Rudd is alive & doing it

VIETCONG AL FATAH BLACK PANTHERS YOUTH INTERNATIONAL PARTY TUPAMAROS YOUNG LORDS PATHET LAO WEATHERMAN RED GUARD FUERZAS ARMADAS REVOLUCIONARIAS MIR REVOLUTIONARY FORCE 9 BLACK LIBERATION FRONT ZENGA KURAN

FUSELESS MOLOTOV:

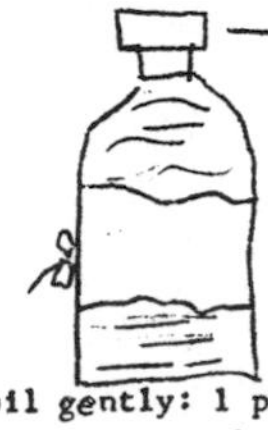

to throw from middle of demonstrations when people trash and fight pigs...(stick it under the wheels of a pig car)

boil gently: 1 part potassium chlorate, 1 part sugar, 2 parts water; soak rag in mixxture--wrap around bottle

MATCHBOOK FIRES:

place a lit cigarette in a book of matches; leave on combustible material.

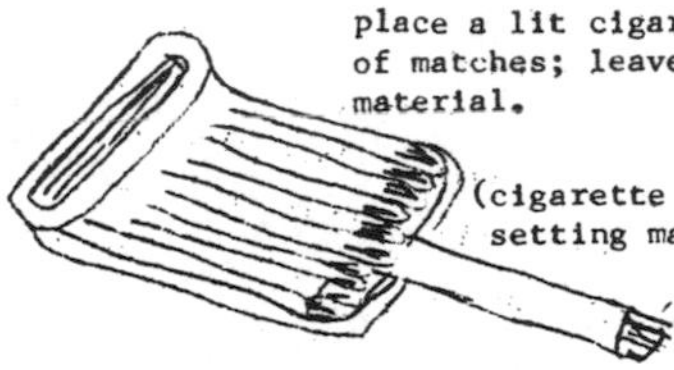

to put in garbage, trash cans, or in pockets of clothes in department stores, trashcans on the street, etc.

STERNO INCENDIARY BOMB:

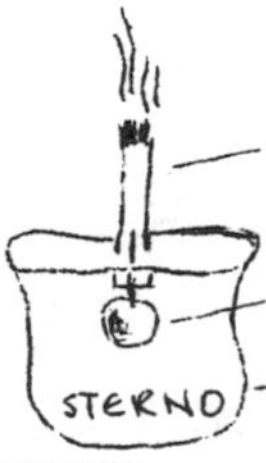

throw as a firebomb through windows, use in demonstrations, leave in easily-burnable buildings, near papers, etc.

CAUTIONS:

1. Test each part of each device separately and progressively together until device is completed; test each completed device before using it.
2. Wear plastic gloves when making bombs and gloves when placing or throwing it--NO FINGERPRINTS, NO DIRECT EVIDENCE.
3. Wash devices down with alcohol when finished, remove fingerprints.

Get M-80's and cherry bombs in Pennsylvania, W. Virginia, Ohio, Washington, D. C.

memorize and burn this leaflat!!

YOUTH, CLASS, AND PARTY

• A TALK ON THE RELATIONSHIP OF YOUNG REVOLUTIONISTS TO THE WORKING CLASS AND THE REVOLUTIONARY PARTY.

• GIVEN BY–

REVOLUTIONARY COMMUNIST YOUTH

The RCY bases itself on the political and organizational ideas of Marx, Lenin, and Trotsky. As the youth section of the Spartacist League, and in political solidarity with it, we reject the idea that students or youth as such can play the vanguard revolutionaryrole. The RCY works as a disciplined part of the revolutionary movement as a whole. We seek to assist in the building of a revolutionary vanguard party <u>of the working class</u> to lead the struggle here and internationally for a successful socialist revolution, which will lay the basis for freeing the energies of all of humanity in a true communist society.

• thursday, 12 noon
july 13 305 finley

CCNY
REVOLUTIONARY
COMMUNIST
YOUTH (RCY)

INFORMATION: 925-2426

Appendix IV

Excerpt from the Minutes of the Meeting of the Faculty Senate of City College, February 18, 1971

Professor Adelson objected to the publication in the minutes of the meeting of January 14 of the resolution introduced by the Executive Committee which took exception to the quotations from Professors Adelson and Heller in the syndicated column of Evans and Novak on open admissions. The secretary explained that the original text was needed to explain the debate as outlined in the minutes, since the revised form of the resolution as passed did not do so. Professor Silver denounced its inclusion, the treatment of the debate in the minutes, and other shortcomings of Senate secretarial reporting. He moved to delete the phrase "it would not affect jobs and promotions" and to add fuller explanation for Professor Arrowsmith's reference to the Reichstag trials. The motion was defeated. Professor Adelson moved to strike from the minutes the original resolution introduced by the Executive Committee. The motion was defeated. Professor Adelson contended that the Executive Committee's resolution had been out of order in the first place since it had not been mentioned in the agenda but had been introduced as part of the report of that committee. Provost Schwartz ruled that the Executive Committee may introduce motions since it carries on the business of the Senate between meetings. Professors Adelson's challenge to this ruling engendered some discussion, following which it was defeated. The minutes of the meeting of January 14 were approved as amended.